LOSE YOUR OLD SCISSORS

52 Blocks to build the Castle of Personal Productivity

P.S.Satish

Chennai • Bangalore

CLEVER FOX PUBLISHING
Chennai, India

Published by CLEVER FOX PUBLISHING 2023
Copyright © P.S.Satish 2023

All Rights Reserved.
ISBN: 978-93-56489-02-8

This book has been published with all reasonable efforts taken to make the material error-free after the consent of the author. No part of this book shall be used, reproduced in any manner whatsoever without written permission from the author, except in the case of brief quotations embodied in critical articles and reviews.

The Author of this book is solely responsible and liable for its content including but not limited to the views, representations, descriptions, statements, information, opinions and references ["Content"]. The Content of this book shall not constitute or be construed or deemed to reflect the opinion or expression of the Publisher or Editor. Neither the Publisher nor Editor endorse or approve the Content of this book or guarantee the reliability, accuracy or completeness of the Content published herein and do not make any representations or warranties of any kind, express or implied, including but not limited to the implied warranties of merchantability, fitness for a particular purpose. The Publisher and Editor shall not be liable whatsoever for any errors, omissions, whether such errors or omissions result from negligence, accident, or any other cause or claims for loss or damages of any kind, including without limitation, indirect or consequential loss or damage arising out of use, inability to use, or about the reliability, accuracy or sufficiency of the information contained in this book.

Dedication

To my loving

wife, Janaki

son, Sanjay

daughter-in-law, Deeksha and

daughter, Sanjana.

CONTENTS

Foreword vi
Acknowledgements x
Preface and Introduction xii

1. Power Of Taking Actions 1
2. Harness The Power Of Thinking 5
3. Setting Your Priorities 9
4. Decide To Decide 14
5. Facing Challenges 18
6. No Problem Is A Problem 22
7. Excuses – Killer Of Personal Productivity 26
8. Developing A Change Mindset 30
9. Be Proactive 34
10. Power In Question 38
11. Overcome Procrastination 42
12. Learn To Learn 47
13. Avoid Multitasking 52
14. Work On Your Interpersonal Skills 56
15. Lose Your Old Scissors 60
16. Work Towards The Goal 64
17. Past – Present – Future 68
18. Do Not Be A Perfectionist 72
19. Develop Kaizen Mindset 76
20. Attitude Towards Your Work 80
21. Learn To Say 'No' 84
22. Develop Good Habits 88
23. Schedule Your Tasks 92
24. Master The Art Of Delegation 96

25. Learn the Power of Focus 100
26. Work On Your Health To Be Productive 104
27. Your Daily Reflections 108
28. Express Gratitude 112
29. Face Fear And Anxiety 116
30. My Ten Personal Productivity Practices 120
31. Be Organized 124
32. Effective Usage Of Your Time 128
33. Are You Feeling Fulfilled? 132
34. Managing Your Emails 136
35. Control Your Thoughts 140
36. Be Like Bees 144
37. Productivity In Oral Communication 148
38. Do You Work Like A Hare Or Tortoise? 152
39. Limit Your Overthinking 156
40. Make A Wonderful Day 160
41. Manage Conflicts Constructively 164
42. Work On Unproductive Forces 168
43. Change Your Perspective 172
44. Four I's Of The Leader 176
45. Mobile And Social Media As Enablers 180
46. Know The Path And Walk The Path 184
47. Increase Roti Of The Meetings 188
48. Ways to Overcome Negativity 193
49. Cling to Routines 197
50. Overcoming Laziness 201
51. Do Not Lose the Person 205
52. Take Responsibility 209

Epilogue *213*
Profile of the Author, P. S. Satish *215*

FOREWORD

It is my pleasure to write this preface for my good old friend's new creation, *Lose Your Old Scissors – 52 Blocks to build the Castle of Personal Productivity.*

I have known Satish both professionally and personally for over 3 decades. I had the privilege to see him closely working on various projects related to technology. During my long professional career at an international level, we had many crossroads where I discovered the critical eye that he has been gifted with. His passion for continuous improvement in whatever field he worked was clearly evident in his acts.

When Satish began his journey as an independent consultant, he probably got a bigger opportunity to practice what he learned throughout his long professional career. Satish has been an excellent coach, mentor, technical expert and, finally a great human being. His several creations in teaching society at large are a testimony of his dedication and commitment to giving back to society. He is currently associated with my organization to coach some of my very senior executives and is an important stakeholder in steering our strategy journey at Auto Ignition Limited (AUTO-LEK).

Satish has authored several articles focussing on various aspects of the current challenges the industry is facing—each one of them being extremely unique in its approach. He has published books related to the power of actions and developing entrepreneurial thinking. He has trained hundreds of professionals with his long and rich industry experience. I am happy to write a foreword for this book. We had a great conversation when he told me about his intentions to write this book. He specifically wanted to emphasize the importance of personal productivity for the success of any industry and, at the same time, talk about how it can help individuals and their families at large to lead a successful life. His request to me to write a foreword for this book makes me proud and gives me a chance to uncover the real thoughts of the author from an external perspective.

We all know that we are living in an age of disruption. Many experts call it an era of exponential growth for the industry. The highly competitive global scenario, especially with reference to the technological hegemony in every field, including space or military research, is significantly impacting the economic equation between different parts of the world. To succeed in this aspiration, it is simply not enough to work on scientific and technological innovations. In addition, a country must nurture and protect the developed technology for a long period of time. The modern technological hegemony has a strong influence not only from mastering the complexity of technology development but also the national productivity, seamless supply chain and speed to market. In all these developments, individuals play a vital role. Needless to say, Satish's focus on achieving high personal productivity in this book makes it a wonderful read for every professional for practicing in real life.

The fundamental instinct of the human race to enhance the "satisfaction of living" has been the driver since the Stone Age that motivated humans to innovate and develop technologies centuries over centuries. We all know the success story of a small country like Israel that has made miracles in farming by increasing output by 26% while reducing water consumption by 12% in a span of 10 years. Such miraculous results are only possible through a focused approach to increasing productivity and simultaneously reducing waste. When I look back on my own journey of corporate experience, the results that looked impossible to achieve have now been superseded with new records. The only thing that I can firmly say today is that no goal is impossible, and no journey has a destination. The harder you work towards a target, the more aspirational you get about setting a new target.

During one of my visits to Taiwan a few years ago, I had an amazing experience with Taiwan's overall productivity levels. One of my organizers made a day's schedule to visit at least 3 companies at 3 different locations. It involved road travel as well as train travel. The focus on productivity was evident at every stage of my journey—be it having lunch, the discipline of train timings, the efficiency of carrying out factory visits, business discussions and many other aspects. In the entire day's trip of over 10 hours, I simply don't remember if we wasted even one minute due to any reason whatsoever. This experience made a long-lasting impact on my thought process, and I started imagining if we in our country achieve such productivity levels, where would we reach? In my view, besides a collective effort, we all need to introspect about our personal productivity levels, which Satish has meticulously tried to uncover in this book.

When we look holistically at this topic, one cannot ignore the fact that we must constantly be reminded about the problem we are trying to address. For example, man, machine, material, method, customer, supplier, logistics, etc. If we are unable to categorize the exact nature of the problem into a specific bucket, we might run into a circle without finding a solution. One of the most typical scenes at most organizations is the time spent by the management in the meeting rooms discussing solutions to problems that are not even defined. We must be able to differentiate between a problem and a symptom. The cost of manhours spent in non-productive ways is one of the biggest wastes for most organizations that completely go unnoticed and unaddressed. Questioning myself as to what value addition is done by me by participating in a group meeting should be a part of self-reflection after every event.

In one of my own research projects, an interesting fact was discovered about white-collar productivity. Most of the white-collar employees were engaged in following up with others or attending meetings where they had nothing much to contribute beyond silent listeners. Over 70% of the staff admitted that they are mostly silent listeners with no value addition. The core work of "making improvement and creativity" fell in the smallest of the pie for most of the executives. The important point is whether this situation is by choice or compulsion.

Multi-tasking in today's world, seen as highly productive, can be detrimental to a specific focus. This book talks about the flip sides of multi-tasking and suggests ways to deal. Organizations must try to provide opportunities for every employee to develop lateral skills that will help them grow as well as learn.

The journey into the space of productivity is not just challenging but equally interesting. Worldwide, people are working on it continuously with better tools such as digitalization and IoT to achieve better results for their organizations. In this new age of global interconnectivity and interdependence, it is necessary to have a collaborative approach to learn faster for better results in a shorter time. Satish's painstaking efforts in articulating his thoughts in this book are a big step in that direction.

I am confident every reader of this book will not only get richer in knowledge, but this reading experience will also provide an essential recipe for a more fulfilling and successful life.

Rajendra Abhange
President and CEO,
Autoignition Limited,
Pirthla, Haryana, India

ACKNOWLEDGEMENTS

I acknowledge, with gratitude, many authors and writers who have inspired me with their thoughts. I have benefited from reading their work and have used them appropriately in the book, with the sole idea that many more can benefit from them.

I acknowledge many friends, associates, all participants of my training sessions and my customers who shared their thoughts, experiences, problems, and views on personal productivity through face–to–face, e-mail, LinkedIn, and WhatsApp.

Thanks to those who pushed me to bring out this fourth book. Without their subtle pressure, I would not have given serious thought to this.

I appreciate the support of my family members while writing this book. They have demonstrated a lot of patience by listening to some of the draft paragraphs of this book and offering corrections.

I am indebted to my good friend Rajendra Abhange, President and CEO of Auto Ignition Limited, Pirthla, Haryana, India, who was kind enough to write the foreword for the book, adding his experience on the topic this book deals with.

Rajendra Abhange is a Fellow in Mechanical Engineering (FIE) and a Certified Chartered Engineer (CE) having core strengths in automotive business management, strategic leadership (Oxford), customer relationship, new business acquisition, product technology, innovation, human resource, lean manufacturing, and operations. His industry experience spans over 36 years in Production Planning, Operations, Strategic Projects,

Technology Transfer, Product Strategy, Industry Automation Human Resources, and many other leadership roles. He has several technology patents and has earned National Awards, including the most prestigious *"Golden Peacock Eco-Innovation Award"* in 2012 and *"Arch of Excellence"* Award in 2014. He is a global-level speaker, often conducting workshops on futuristic technologies such as e-mobility, autonomous driving, system safety engineering and advanced suspension.

I acknowledge the encouragement and motivation of members (called Learners) of a WhatsApp group I curated, 'LEARNERS GROUP'.

I am grateful to my parents, teachers, mentors, and hundreds of others who taught me about life and supported me on my life journey.

I thank Clever Fox Publishing, Bengaluru, for their dedicated efforts to bring out the book on time and quality with their guidance in publishing.

PREFACE AND INTRODUCTION

As a corporate trainer and mentor to manufacturing industries, I have had the opportunity to interact with hundreds of companies and people. Helping people to develop themselves is one of my passions, and I use every occasion I get to guide, coach and mentor those who are really interested in their personal development. I share things which have worked well for me over the years. I am a strong believer that the growth of a business can happen and be sustained for a long time only by focusing on developing people in terms of enhancing competencies, instilling the ability to think differently and overcoming the limitations each one has set for themselves.

During the Covid pandemic, when most of us were at home, I had an opportunity to conduct a sixteen-hour online program titled *'Personal Productivity for Progress.'* The participants shared many benefits from this program, which in turn triggered me to think about writing a book on personal productivity adding many other aspects.

The various topics I used with my participants and mentees, for them to be more productive personally, are summarised in this book. I wish many people read, reflect, and apply the topics or ideas that work for them. When we have more productive people, who are conscious of their time, their flow of energy and priorities, and work continuously to improve themselves, we will see a better world.

In this competitive world, there is a need for business entities and individuals to be better than what they were yesterday. To decrease costs and be competitive, we must focus on productivity constantly. For companies, it is about increasing the output from the company with the same or reduced input. The productivity of a company can be loosely defined as the collective productivity of all people involved. Productivity is a measure of the efficiency of a person, machine, system and so on in converting inputs into useful outputs.

At the individual level, a doubt that may pop up is about the benefit one will get by being more productive. There are two benefits. The first one is that your output will increase for the given efforts and time spent. High targets can be achieved in a shorter period of time. The second one is that, to get the same output, your efforts, mainly time, will be reduced. You will achieve more success. Continued success is possible by striving to be a better version of yourself on a daily basis. One gets more fulfilled by making the best use of their potential.

Focus on technical skills is needed and crucial for your success in your career and business. But that alone is not enough. Non-technical or soft skills are equally important as they will contribute to the change of thinking, better usage of resources, and enhanced inter personal relationship , which in turn leads to higher productivity. The business will grow to the extent the employees think and grow.

Personal productivity is about organizing your time, energy, priority, schedule, efforts, and focus to move with ease towards your goals. It is about getting higher value as the outcome for your tasks than completing the tasks. Focus on personal productivity is one of the foundation blocks for success. Benefits include the ability to achieve more, reach the goal faster, enhanced quality of work, less stress, more fulfilment, less firefighting and enhanced capacity to take up more responsibilities. Personal productivity relates more towards accomplishments than just doing. Being busy is not productive. Thinking about why to be busy, busy for what, and what will come out of it can be productive.

With more output, you are recognized better and it opens doors for further opportunities. You will feel satisfied and proud of your achievements. You qualify yourself for taking up more responsibilities, which is very important in the industry and corporate world.

Many times, personal productivity is linked to time management. No doubt, using time is important. But at the same time, we have to look at the intensity while using this time. Intensity includes the right priority, mindset, energy level, emotional level, attention and focus without disturbance and so on. Working on a task using both time and intensity leads to higher productivity.

The leadership journey starts with self-awareness and improving oneself. Personal productivity helps to lead oneself better, to enable leading others and, later, the situation or community.

With the extra time you get, by being personally productive, you can pursue your hobbies, go on vacations, spend more time with family and friends, read a book, focus on improving your health, engage in some social activity, or take up any additional job to add to your earnings. In short, your efforts will be used in the best way.

Being effective and efficient

Having understood the definition of productivity as a ratio of output to input, you can focus on two areas to be more productive. One area is focusing on increasing the output or results. When output is achieved or exceeded, then you are said to be more effective. The second area is focusing on the input in terms of reducing time or effort. You are said to be efficient when you focus on reducing the input without caring about the output. When output as well as input requirements are achieved, i.e., when you get the result with reasonable efforts, you are said to be efficient and effective.

Here is an example to distinguish between effectiveness and efficiency. Suppose a courier is to be delivered to a customer by next Tuesday. You can send it by express courier by paying premium charges to ensure it reaches on Tuesday or earlier. Then, you are effective but not efficient. Instead, you use a normal post to save your efforts and money, but if the courier reaches later than Tuesday, then you are efficient and not effective. When you ensure that the courier reaches on Tuesday, by proper planning and execution, with a normal post, then you are effective and efficient. Personal productivity is about increasing the output as well as decreasing the input.

The book covers 52 chapters, elaborating on various ways through which personal productivity can be enhanced. Each small chapter gives an overview. 52 signifies the number of weeks in a year, suggesting the need for practice throughout the year, with one topic per week. You can expand your knowledge and skill about the topic of each chapter by further reading.

There are a few topics related to the mind, such as the power of thinking, working on thoughts, facing fears and anxiety, related to mindset and so on. I must admit that I am not a psychologist. These are written from my experience of seeing people around me and the knowledge I have gained over a period. To go deeper into topics related to the mind, readers are requested to consult a trained professional in the area.

The right way to get benefits from the book

The fact that you have picked this book to read indicates that you have some inclination towards improving your personal productivity. I appreciate your decision. Congratulations on taking the first step—the most important one for success and to improve. The first step always leads to the next one.

If one wants to be successful in their chosen career, both competence and commitment are required. The book supports readers to reflect on these compared to their current level and to work further on these two elements.

I do not recommend any specific sequence in which this book should be read, as each chapter is independent. A doctor gives a combination of drugs depending on the disease of the patient. There is no single drug which cures all diseases and for all patients. Likewise, a combination of a few chapters may work best for you. I suggest you read the book thoroughly once and mark the chapters that resonate with you. In the second round, go deeper to reflect and identify the gap, and write down your insights and actions you want to take at the end of each chapter. Highlight sentences and words that will reinforce your thinking. Review the status of your committed actions and the results you get after three months. Reading a few times with a little gap in between is suggested for better absorption since all topics are soft in nature. Since topics are related to soft skills, consistent practice of knowledge gained is needed to derive full benefit.

The shorter the gap between identifying the need for the action and acting, the better the results will be. Talk to your friend about your findings or insights and share your learnings. I suggest reading the book once a year to review your overall progress and explore new actions.

Any idea or insight, if not written down, will be lost quickly. It could even change your thinking. Even a tiny action taken can give lot of dividends. Drops of water create an ocean over a period. Good seeds must be nurtured by watering and preparing the soil by giving light and manure to grow into a healthy tree.

Thoughts are like seeds and practicing self-development is like nurturing them. Consider this a workbook for self-development.

Only reading for the sake of knowledge and not applying it to real-life scenarios will not benefit you fully. Practicing with fundamental understanding is the only key to success. Paint in a Paintbox is not much of use unless applied in the right proportion, in the right way, and in the right thickness at the right place.

Any book is like a signpost indicating ways to the destination. You will benefit only by walking along the path towards the destination through regular practice, as given in the book, and, over a period, many things will become part of you.

Remember the words of Tony Robbins, American writer and motivational speaker, "It's not what we do occasionally that shapes our lives. It's what we do consistently." Practice will condition your mind to repeat actions with minimum effort.

With humility, I recommend you read my other books: *Knowing Is Not Same as Doing* and *The Great Entrepreneur Blueprint – 52 Dimensions'* (both available on Amazon, Flipkart and Jio e-platforms).

Happy reading. Enjoy the beautiful journey of personal productivity. Work on being a better version of yourself.

1

POWER OF TAKING ACTIONS

The price of inaction is far greater than the cost of a mistake

– Meg Whitman

A pinch of application is worth tons of abstraction. Your intention has no meaning unless it is followed up with actions. Who you are is decided not by your intentions but by what you do. Emphasising actions, Brendon Burchard, performance coach and New York best-selling author, said, "We must remember we are not the sum of our intentions but of our actions." Reflect on whether you are an action-taker or action-talker. No amount of plan, strategy, goal setting and action plan has meaning unless efforts are taken for the meticulous execution of actions. Action is not just about movement or keeping busy with a task. By the power of taking actions, I mean those actions that have a great impact on the goal and results. Doing is engaging in an activity, but action has a purpose.

Output is linked to input or efforts. Efforts are nothing but actions. The more the focus is on increasing the input, the more the output will be. Have you come across people who are grumbling about problems or are struggling to improve? If you go a little deeper with them, you will realise that they will be talking about the situation without taking the number of actions needed.

Decide on the areas you want to care about that will give you joy, happiness and fulfilment. Taking care of those things you care about means taking the necessary actions in those areas. If you care for health, what actions are you taking consistently to maintain and improve your health? Focus on your cares without allowing distractions.

Possible reasons why people hesitate to take actions could be laziness, fear, force of habit or a core belief that actions are of no use. All of your actions may not give the intended results. That is the law of nature. Here, you have the choice of either walking away or trying harder with a different approach. Do not give up; continue to take the next actions. Remember that anything we do has a 10% success rate, and 90% is failure. So, take lessons from failures and attempt 10 times to be successful. A winner is just a loser who tried one more time.

When you fail in an action to get the intended results, whether you will take the next action or stop acting depends on what thoughts you entertain when you are not successful. Suppose you miss a catch in a cricket game, a few thoughts that might come to you are, "Cricket is tough," or "I am not good at catching," or "I am not meant to be a cricketer," or "I am not able to master this," or "I am good for nothing" and so on. These disempowering thoughts support you to stop taking appropriate actions. Replace empowering thoughts like, "By missing a catch, I know where I should focus," or "This gave me an opportunity to learn new things," or "I have to train myself to be better," and so on, which will motivate you to take the next actions.

The biggest wall you must climb is the one created in your mind. The mental blocks that stop you from taking action are previous attempts that did not work out, earlier rejections, escape from reality, poor self-image, blaming others and lack of commitment. Unless you first take action to remove these mental blocks, you will encounter challenges to take the next actions.

If you attach too much meaning to what happened in the past, you may see the future from the past perspective and not from the present one. The result may be that the future turns out to be the same as the past. To avoid this, the key is to act now by taking only lessons from the past.

Karma yoga in the holy book, Bhagavad-Gita, talks about attitude towards actions. It says that you have control over the actions and not on the results. It does not mean that you should not work for the results. It means that you must do your best and accept the results that come out. Also, it says that actions are to be done in the form of service or surrender. Mother serving food to children considers her actions as service, and she will never get tired.

Avoid too much of actions on one care by neglecting others. It may lead to burn out. Act on care like physical, mental, spiritual, emotional, financial, social, relationship, hobby and so on. To make your actions more meaningful, ask yourself every hour, "Is what I am doing meaningful? Am I taking care of my cares? Am I really focused?"

"The cave you fear to enter holds the treasure you seek," said Joseph Campbell, an American writer. Be ready to leave your comfort zone and take actions you are not comfortable with. The comfort zone is your enemy, and you must push yourself to the growth zone. Be comfortable to be uncomfortable.

In one of the trainings, the trainer showed a picture of a stopped car and asked why the car stopped. Everyone gave many probable reasons like no fuel, battery dead, engine problem, heavy traffic, flat tire and so on. Finally, the trainer said that the actual reason was that the driver stopped pressing the accelerator pedal. Are you familiar with this? You expect the project to move without pressing the accelerator pedal; that is taking action.

Reduce the gap between sensing and responding. If you sense a toothache, will you go to the doctor to get treated immediately? Consequences may be high in delaying the action after sensing. Responding immediately after sensing is an important aspect of risk management. Godzilla is a fictional monster. It was a cute baby and grew to destroy the city. The moral of this is to act on small problems when sensed before they become big.

As per Zen philosophy, jump into action without waiting for a revelation to happen. Your actions will reveal the next action move, and the way will open. Unless you climb the first step, the second one will not be seen. Don't wait for a perfect time to start.

Which action is of the least cost here—inaction, delayed action, hurried action, mechanical action, or thoughtful action? Inaction is very expensive. Take proactive, thoughtful action on things you can control. Move from mindless action to mindful action. Actions are manifestations of what happens inside the mind. To improve the quality of actions, improve the quality of your thinking. To get 10x results, efforts through correct actions should be more than 10x.

Spending time learning and not putting it into practice is a waste of time. Medicines will not work unless you take them. We judge ourselves by our intentions, and others judge us by our actions. Knowing is not the same as doing. Just knowing the path is insufficient; walking the path is progress. Follow the advice of David Schwartz, the motivational speaker, "Be an activationist. Be someone who does things— a doer, not a don't-er." Motivation is a byproduct of taking action. Start taking action in a small way, and you will continue to act, and the momentum builds up this way.

My top three improvement action points

1.
2.
3.

2

HARNESS THE POWER OF THINKING

No problem can withstand the assault of sustained thinking

– Voltaire

Many years back, I stayed in Germany for a few years. I was relatively young at that time and always had some questions to ask. I had a very senior and technically sound person in our department, and I saw that many used to approach him for his advice related to their projects or professions. He was a friendly person, tough, strict, and highly disciplined. I had some dilemma in one of the projects I was working on, and I approached him, of course, with an appointment for a solution. He listened attentively with patience, and I was eager to get a ready capsule from him to solve my issue.

He did not say much while I was talking, and at the end, he said, "Satish, you have all the solutions in your mind. Think over and reflect. You will get it. You can reach out to me again if you do not find it in a few weeks." I was a little bit disappointed with his short answer. Half-heartedly, I started thinking about the problem, its causes and consequences and possible solutions. Over the next few days, I realized that the problem was in my mind, and that led to exaggerating the problem out of proportion. Many times, more than the problem, the way we look at the problem is a problem. My senior was right, and I found the solution by thinking to myself. He was happy to hear that I found a solution on my own, and I thanked him for triggering my thinking.

Thinking consciously about a specific issue or topic is not easy for many. You will find many doers in the organization who are comfortable doing things where thinking is done by others. For the growth of the organization, with dynamic changes happening in the market, more thinkers are needed than doers. In one of the global surveys done by LinkedIn, critical thinking is considered one of the skills needed by employees beyond 2020 to address dynamic changes happening globally like intense competition, competitive pressure, increasing customer demands, technology changes, higher compliance, social changes, volatility, global economy changes and many others.

I applied the lessons learnt from my senior in Germany later in my professional life to a great extent. For some period, I served as an adjunct professor at a university. I used to teach a module to students pursuing their master's degrees. As a part of curricular requirements, students had to do a six-month project in an industry guided by the industry and academic guide. I had opportunities to guide many students. Their job to do a project starts with the selection of the right project. For a few students, this became a challenge as they did not get any clue from their industry.

When they used to approach me with a proposal for their projects, I used the technique that I learnt in Germany by telling them, "If I suggest a project, I know you would do well. Your conviction will be higher if you select. I understand your difficulty finding the right one. I urge you to spend at least 2 hours daily in the library for the next 2-3 weeks looking for potential subjects or projects and thinking over those that can be converted as projects. I will guide you once you have made a selection." To my surprise, it worked well in all the cases where a student had difficulty identifying a project. Initially, their mindset was to look for an easy solution without themselves thinking.

At the end of the preaching of Bhagavad Gita on the battlefield, Arjuna asks Lord Krishna a question, "You have told me everything. Now tell me what I should do next." Krishna didn't want to spoon-feed Arjuna and told him, "Do what you think is right." The message here is that even the Lord wants thinkers and not doers as per the instructions.

Brian P Morgan and Michael Lennington, in their book *Uncommon Accountability*, bring out a model called RAT to get better results. As per them, the results (R) you create are the outcome of your actions (A) which comes from thinking (T) which in turn is the summation of your fear, habits, values, feelings, experience, and knowledge. The summary is that thinking drives behaviours that create results. Thinking is a combination of your unconscious beliefs and dynamic conscious thoughts.

The Flynn effect, named after Jim Flynn, says that the IQ of people has grown over centuries. One of the reasons attributed is that over the period, jobs and daily lives ask people to think more logically and analytically. Schools are encouraging students to learn more reasoning by thinking than through memorising.

How do you incorporate the practice of intentional thinking? Allocate 'thinking time' in your daily schedule. Use that time to think about the aspects that went by, the lessons learnt and the ways to incorporate them in the following days. Thinking may include planning for the future, improvements, reflections on the way projects are going, self-development plans and so on. You will not get time for this important activity unless you make time for it. Otherwise, today will be eaten by yesterday's and today's problems, leaving no room to solve tomorrow's problems, and tomorrow will be the same as yesterday.

To bring practice or culture of thinking in the organization, encourage employees to form small groups within or across the department and spend some time together with a definite frequency to think on specific key topics related to the function, department, or organization. Every thought you think up is creating a future. To address a problem, to improve or to change a situation, start thinking differently. Until you change your thinking, you will always be recycling your experiences. Happy thinking.

My top three improvement action points

1.

2.

3.

3

SETTING YOUR PRIORITIES

The key is not to prioritize what's on your schedule, but to schedule your priorities
                                                    – Stephen Covey

Productivity is not about doing things meticulously but deciding what must be done first and what must not be done at all. It is about doing the right things. Being busy is not productive. The question to ask yourself is, "Busy for what?" Do not get into the 'busy trap'. Motion is not progress. Everyone on this earth has only 24 hours per day. But successful people can accomplish more in this span than many others do. The secret lies in their ability to take up tasks of the highest importance and priority.

Tim Ferris, in his book 'Tools of Titan' says how people use the pretext of being busy, "Being busy is most often used as a guise for avoiding the few critically important but uncomfortable actions."

About priority, Stephen Covey, the American Educator, says, "When you have too many top priorities, you effectively have no top priority." Before scheduling an activity, decide on the priority. Activities are different from accomplishments. Set your priorities of activities to accomplish more in the given time. Activities are a means to an end and not the end by themselves.

List down all the pending tasks and other things you want to initiate this week. How did you prepare? How many are important in this list? How many are linked to the target you want to achieve? What are your top priorities for tomorrow? Realize that not all the tasks on your 'to-do list' are of equal importance.

Some possible ways you might pick up a job:
- easy jobs first before the difficult ones
- tackle first what is known before unknown ones
- tackle first the one you like the most
- complete those tasks first that take less time
- respond first to the demands of others before what you want to do
- focus on urgent things without scheduling important items
- wait for a deadline to approach and start doing in last minute
- respond based on who wants it
- work on things as they arrive
- interesting ones before taking up uninteresting ones
- complete small jobs first to tick more items in the to-do list
- do things by habit without looking at the sequence
- do when it becomes a crisis
- attend to those who make a noise, and so on.

By taking up the activities like these which keep you occupied, do you think you can be productive? Reflect deeply to realise the importance of setting priorities.

Before climbing the tree, decide if it is worth climbing. Before picking up a task, ask these questions to yourself: Should I do this? Why? How will it help me to move towards my goal? Can someone else do it for me? Should I do it now or delay it?

Tasks can be grouped mainly into two categories: urgent and important. Urgent ones are driven by deadlines, crises, pressing problems, emergencies and so on. Important ones are preventive in nature and involve activities like planning, competency building, creating opportunities, recreation and so on

Further combination of urgent and important tasks leads to a matrix with four quadrants, as defined in the well-known Eisenhower Matrix, and its corresponding actions:
- Urgent and important –DO IT NOW
- Not urgent but important – PLAN IT
- Urgent but not important – DELEGATE
- Not urgent and not important – DUMP IT

Make time to do activities of importance instead of trying to do them when you find time. Daily exercise and reading are not urgent but important for growth. Unlike urgent things, important things are normally postponed as you do not feel the impact now.

Priority is about giving prior attention over other things and doing what is right and not what is easy. Brian Tracy, a Canadian-American motivational speaker, recommends starting the day with tough jobs, ones that need full attention instead of easy ones. In his words, 'Eat ugly frogs first.' If you start the day with easy jobs, you may not have time to accommodate difficult ones later.

The Pareto principle says that 80% of results are achieved by focusing on 20% of items. Priority is about identifying those vital 20% and scheduling them. If you start filling the jar with sand first, you cannot accommodate pebbles and stones later. Trivial things are like the sand. Set high priority for jobs that you tend to postpone, which are critical for the results, which are difficult, and which take effort and time.

Actions are different from significant actions. Significant actions, unlike actions, are critical and more focused; by doing that, you progress, feel fulfilled, and move towards your goal faster. What significant actions do you want to take up tomorrow? Ivy Lee suggests a way to set priorities for tomorrow. Identify six important ones to do and set the sequence of doing. The next day, complete the first task listed fully before going to the next one. Follow the same order of priority. If unfinished, add to the list of six tasks for the next day.

This oxymoron is apt on setting priority, "What is the biggest small thing I can do today?" Ask this question daily, and you will start developing the habit of setting the right priorities.

Trifurcate the tasks that must be done: should do, nice to do and to avoid. What are your must-do lists for the day, the week, and the month? When you plan for the month, set priority for important items like meetings, holidays, family functions, specific project-related, self-development and innovative tasks. Bring those items to a weekly schedule and later to daily.

James clearly talks about the practice of priority by focused people, "Highly focused people do not leave their options open. They select their priorities and are comfortable ignoring the rest. If you commit to nothing, you will be distracted by everything."

Follow the 4Ds for your tasks and corresponding possible actions:
- **D**o – Schedule and keep a reminder for a follow-up in the timeline.
- **D**elegate – To whom, how and when?
- **D**efer – Till when? Review often.
- **D**ump – Delete.

For productivity, the balance between doing things right and doing the right things is important. Before doing a task, ask yourself what Stephen Covey, American Writer, said, "Are you cutting the wrong tree efficiently?'. Deciding on the right priority will enable you to spend more time on things that matter the most to you. You will never have time to do it until you make it a priority.

My top three improvement action points

1.

2.

3.

4

DECIDE TO DECIDE

It does not take much strength to do things, but it requires great strength to decide what to do
— **Chow Ching**

Decision-making is about choosing among various alternatives. The word 'decide' has a Latin origin, meaning killing alternatives or options. Have you come across people who are energetic to talk about plans, intentions, and goals but struggle to decide to take the next step? Decision-making is one of the key competencies needed for success, especially for a leader. Your lack of decision-making ability will demotivate your team, and progress will be hampered. Nothing happens till a decision is made. A decision is a spark that ignites action. When you decide, be ready to lose something in order to get something else.

You must have heard the fable of Buridan's donkey. It was equally thirsty and hungry. It was placed precisely midway between hay and water. The donkey could not choose between these two and died of hunger and thirst. We find many around us who find it difficult to decide. If you are in a situation where all options look the same, decide on the one with fewer negatives.

Why do many have difficulty making a decision? Possible reasons could be fear of failure, not being ready to face the new situation, change will bring in a lot of effort, fear of losing existing position, laziness, procrastination tendencies, looking for an ideal condition to start, trying to be in the comfort zone, averse to taking any risk, not ready to sacrifice something when all options look equal or lack of sufficient information.

If there are no choices, it is easy to decide. It may not be so always. When you do not decide, you are deciding to allow things to happen in their own way. When you don't decide, someone else may decide for you, which may not be in your favour. Take control by making decisions yourself. Your life will get better only when you decide to get better. Every decision you take by selecting among choices has consequences including those which you have not decided by not selecting. Many times, the negative consequence of no decision may be higher than making a wrong decision. If you decide, you may go wrong. By not deciding, you will lose the potential opportunity in store.

All your decisions may not get the expected results. Better to take a faster decision. If you are failing, fail fast. At least you gain time to correct and try again differently. Delayed decisions can be costly. At the same time, for the sake of taking a decision, do not make a reckless decision without giving adequate thought.

In 1998, Yahoo had the opportunity to buy the upcoming search engine Google for 1 Million Dollars but did not go further. In 2002, Yahoo realised its mistake and offered to buy at 3 billion dollars. Google demanded 5 billion dollars, and the deal didn't go through. In 2008, Microsoft offered 40 billion dollars to Yahoo to take over. Yahoo refused, and in 2016, Verizon bought Yahoo for 4.6 billion dollars. What went wrong? Is there something to look at the decision-making capability of Yahoo? Is it a consequence of not making timely decisions by those involved?

In some cases, you have to choose to do something instead of deciding. In decision, you select based on a few criteria or alternatives, but in choice, you select because you want it. To be happy, choose to be happy instead of deciding to be happy. I left the corporate world and chose to be a corporate trainer and mentor because I wanted to be so.

To what extent data is important in decision-making? Though data-driven decisions may not guarantee the right results, they are better than opinions, assumptions, and gut feelings. It is also called a fact-based approach. At the beginning of my career, one of the start-up companies with which I worked had to close down because they made decisions based on assumptions that were not validated with data.

It is said that you are not a loser with a decision. With the right decision, your confidence will increase, and with the wrong decision, your experience will increase. An effective decision is about considering various scenarios and alternatives with data and on time. Even a correct decision is wrong when it is delayed. It may include a portion of assumptions and risks. Your future depends on what you decide today. If you look retrospectively, many decisions were right at that point and may seem wrong from today's standpoint. Do not regret your wrong decisions. Take lessons from it and move on.

Wrong decisions can happen because of insufficient data, hurry, wrong judgements, fear, mind block, emotions, problems or issues not analysed properly, and lack of capability to decide. Blaming others for your wrong decision is the height of immaturity. Stand by your decision and take accountability for your actions and decisions.

To get the best results and progress, all three types of decisions are to be focused on. Operational decisions are related to day-to-day tasks, tactical decisions are related to the medium-term, and strategic decisions are long-term, which involve huge impact. Balancing these three, in the right amount, is the key.

Decisions taken with negative emotions are to be avoided as they will be driven by your mind more than your intellect. Consequences from such decisions may not be favourable and can be damaging and regrettable.

Decisions bring clarity, which is the power to take actions which lead to better results. Your destiny is shaped by the decisions you take. If you have made a bad decision, do not try to cover up with another bad decision. If it cannot be rectified with the right decision, it is better to face the consequences.

In an organization, decisions made based on the consensus of the people involved, wherever applicable, give a better result. The Japanese are good at this. You may take time to decide with deliberations, but once decided, execute quickly.

Two decision styles can be applied depending on the situation: Thinker's style, where the decision is arrived with facts and evidence, and Feeler's style, based on how you feel about the problem, situation, or challenge. Decide to move forward and make progress.

My top three improvement action points

1.
2.
3.

5
FACING CHALLENGES

A feeling of confidence and personal power comes from facing challenges and overcoming them
— **Brian Tracy**

There will always be tough times, challenges, and difficulties in the path of life. But facing them will make you stronger, more responsible and prepare yourself to win against all odds. Challenges are opportunities to transform yourself and are one of your greatest teachers. Adversity is a part of life, and facing them is the art of life.

If you are not facing any challenges or problems in your personal and professional life, please think about whether you are attempting enough. Challenges may be posed by situations that you do not create. Addressing them is one aspect. More importantly, challenges that support your growth are those you create by stretching yourself and taking risks. Difficulties are not meant to destroy your life but to help you realise your hidden potential. Smooth seas do not make skilful sailors.

Challenges are situations that need a lot of mental and physical effort to deal with. It may test your ability and potential to tackle them. It can create a lot of stress and depression, may have a high impact, and dealing with them may not be easy.

Negative things are bound to happen. It is not in your control. The most important aspect of dealing with them is having the right mindset. You cannot handle a negative situation with a negative mindset. By changing the language to yourself, a positive framework is possible. Instead of saying, "Challenges are pain," you can say, "Challenges are testing my capability and are an opportunity to learn." Similarly, replace 'difficult' with 'more efforts are required to deal with it' and replace 'failures' with 'learning opportunities'. Your positive language to your mind creates positive emotions, which will drive you to take positive actions.

Challenges could be at a personal level, like losing a job, severe health issues, deep financial loss, failures, loss of loved ones, natural calamities like rain, COVID-19 and so on. At the business level, challenges can be posed by situations of external competition, staying competitive, compliance issues, project deadlines and other market dynamics. Expect unexpected things to come up and mentally be ready to face them boldly. Work on your adversity quotient (AQ). It is an ability to bounce back quickly when there is a setback from challenges.

What are the options available to you for facing challenges? The first one is fear, and with this, you will simply suffer without doing anything to overcome it. The second one is flight, or running away from challenges. The third option is to feign or pretend as if everything is fine when it is obvious that things are not. The fourth option is to fight blindly. The final and best option is to face them with faith, imagining the positive results and with the right actions.

Challenges and setbacks may cause pain. But suffering from pain is your choice. For setbacks, if you start finding meaning or creating internal stories like, 'My bad luck,' 'Why does it happen only to me,' 'My life is gone', and so on, you will suffer much more. Pain is one arrow. When it hits, instead of removing it, if you suffer with meanings, you are allowing another hundred arrows to hit you.

Problems and challenges are like your washing machines. It will twist you, tumble you, squeeze you and spin you, but in the end, you will come out cleaner and brighter than before. Let your difficulties know that you are difficult to handle. Your struggles today are like your daily exercises, which will develop the strength needed tomorrow. Coal cannot become a diamond in an easy route. Develop the mindset and attitude that problems and challenges are not bad, not meant to cause pain & suffering, and they have their contribution in making you strong.

T Harv Eker, author and motivational speaker, recommends embracing challenges by saying, "If you are willing to do only what is easy, life will be hard. But if you are willing to do what is hard, life will be easy." If you are ready to face them, challenges will run away.

If there is a challenge or a problem with no solution, then it is not a problem but a reality to be accepted and learn how to manage it. A few years back, my right knee joint got fractured and it took many months for doctors to make me walk. This led to my physical limitation, which is that I cannot run fast. It is a hard reality, and no amount of grumbling will cure this. I have learnt to live with this, and today, I don't even feel that my knee joint has wires holding it in place.

Reframing to address a challenge can help you to be more positive. In a situation with challenges or in a negative situation, ask yourself reframing questions like, what is good about this? What is it that I should focus on and do now to make it better? What lessons did I learn from this? What is it that I should do differently next time? What skills do I need to develop?

The answer to addressing **challenges** lies in the word itself. That is CHANGE. Challenges are created in the mind. Change your mindset about challenges and how you perceive the situation as opportunities to learn and grow. Change your internal communication from, 'It is a mess' to, 'How can I...?'

"Tough times never last, tough people do," said Robert H Schuller, pastor and author. Be tough and grow bigger than the challenges. Challenges may look heavy, like a big basket of cotton but not so when you start handling it. You can carry more load if you learn how to carry. Difficult times and challenges are sent to promote and strengthen you.

My top three improvement action points

1.
2.
3.

6

NO PROBLEM IS A PROBLEM

The problem isn't the problem. The problem is your attitude about the problem

– Captain Jack Sparrow

Problems are relative. If one perceives something as a problem, another may not feel the same. Everyone will have some sort of problem or other. Those who dare to walk on unknown paths, take up new challenges and dive to explore, will come across more problems. It is said that problems cannot stay alone. It is always associated with a solution. You should develop the mindset to look for solutions and possibilities to resolve the problem. Anything, if focused on, gets magnified. Applicable for problems and solutions as well. Focus on solutions, and you will get it, maybe not immediately, but eventually for sure.

One of the heads of a manufacturing plant meets the company chairman to appraise him on the performance of the plant. The plant head was very excited to present the results as all the numbers were positive, and the results were fantastic.

The chairman asks at the end, "What is the problem?"

The plant head says, "There is no problem."

Now, it was the chairman's turn to say, "That is the problem. No problem is a problem. Look for a problem to solve. Every problem you solve gives you positive opportunities to improve, including enhancing your capability. It gives an opportunity to look from different perspectives, leading to innovation."

Darkness is not the opposite of light; it is the absence of light. Similarly, a problem is not the opposite of a solution; it is the absence of ideas and willingness. Problems are not obstacles, but many times, the way you look at the problems and the lack of your will to resolve them may be the obstacles.

Problems are undecided issues. It is the deviation from the target situations with an unknown cause. If the causes are known, and you are not acting on them, that is the problem of your execution. In engineering quality, problems are defined as something that should not be happening or something that is not happening that should be. Defining exactly and explicitly what the problem is the first step to the solution. Well-defined problems will already have 50% solutions.

None of you know the future of your life or the world. You don't know what problems will come up tomorrow. This is applicable to businesses as well. We are living in a world with high market dynamics, volatility, uncertainty, ambiguity, and complexity. The only way you or your business can solve tomorrow's potential problems is to increase your problem-solving ability within you and your team members. With less capability, problems will grow bigger than you. Be agile and resilient to overcome problems and return to normalcy quickly.

Typical challenges to solving problems for an individual could be a lack of logical thought process, fear of past failures, fear of future failures, lack of self-confidence, tendency to procrastinate, not ready to take action, and not understanding the importance of solving problems.

There are different approaches to solving problems. In the reactive approach, problems are solved after they appear. This is a mindset of waiting for problems to happen before taking action. In the preventive approach, measures are taken to ensure that problems do not reappear. The ideal one would be a proactive approach where problems are anticipated, expecting unexpected things to happen, and solving problems before they appear.

Few mindsets provide support to face and solve problems well. One such mindset by Charles F Kettering, an American inventor, "Don't bring me anything but trouble. Good news weakens me." A few others are, "Problems are inevitable. You cannot avoid them. You can only confront them," "Running away from a problem only increases the distance from the solution," "I take the responsibility to solve my problems," "I look for facts and look for root causes to solve problems," and "I respond to the problem, not react to it." Change the way you look at the problems. It will affect your feelings towards it as well as how you go about fixing it. Perceiving a problem as a problem itself is a problem.

Many suffer from the interpretation of the problem rather than the problem itself. If you lose a job, a few of your interpretations could be, "I am not a capable person," "The world is bad for honest people," "My horoscope and fate are not good," "I am not good enough," "Company is unfair," 'You cannot believe anybody" and so on. When you attach such meanings, it will disempower you, emotionally disturb you, and you may not take the right actions.

To address the problem, how about entertaining empowering thoughts like, "This has allowed me to reflect on areas I need to work on," "It is a lesson I will carry with me to my next job," "I got a break to sharpen my missing skills," "What if I lose a job? The world is big, and I can find another job for sure" and "I should rely on my strengths." Your feelings will improve, leading to better actions with empowering thoughts. Think deeper about the problem and its nature, causes, modes and so on.

In preparation for finding a solution to a problem, Albert Einstein said, "If I had an hour to solve a problem, I'd spend 55 minutes thinking about the problem and 5 minutes thinking about the solution."

In a study in America, one set of students was given easy problems to solve, and the second set was given difficult problems. In the second round, easy and difficult problems were interchanged. The first set of students gave up easily, and the second set of students was far more successful in resolving problems.

Go deeper into the problem to identify the root causes and address them suitably. The goal should be to avoid reoccurrence of the problem. Putting a bandage on the problem to suppress it momentarily, only for it to reappear, is not a good approach.

Do not give up when you don't find a solution to the problem. You may fail many times in resolving. Each step forward brings you closer to the solution. The best triangle to solve a problem is a try-angle.

"No problem can withstand the assault of sustained thinking," as per Voltaire, a French writer. Solving problems makes you fit to solve bigger problems. Don't run away from problems, as opportunities to success come in the disguise of problems. They come as guests in our lives, sign in our logbook of experiences, and move away. Be concerned if you do not have any problems to solve. No problem is a problem.

My top three improvement action points

1.

2.

3.

7

EXCUSES – KILLER OF PERSONAL PRODUCTIVITY

"Ninety-nine percentage of the failures come from people who have the habit of making excuses"
— **George Washington Carver**

As a part of my Sunday sharing session, I recently did an interactive online talk on the topic of personal branding. In earlier sessions, I used to send the online link for the interested ones to join. This time, I sent a registration link via a Google Form for the interested participants to share their contacts and indicate a few questions they might have on the topic to be discussed. I wanted only serious participants. People who attended the program were participative and interactive, which helped me to share the little things I knew and my experiences on the topic. They also expressed the value they got from attending the session.

I noticed that about forty percent of the people who registered independently did not turn up. I respect their decision. There was no message as well on their inability to attend, though registered, on their own. I can understand the other priorities that would have cropped up in the last minutes. There is no issue if it is a genuine reason, beyond control to skip. Being a free program, there was no compulsion for them to attend. Those who registered but did not attend failed on their own commitment. Missing this session might be a very insignificant thing for them, but it has made a dent in their personal branding, which was the essence of the session. After all, personal branding is not about you, but it is how others carry an image of you. Missed ones may come with a lot of excuses, such as forgetting, not setting reminders, realising later that it was Sunday evening, registering to please the speaker but having no intention to attend and so on.

The easiest way to escape commitment is by giving excuses. One way to define an excuse is the gap between what you intend to do and later giving a reason for not doing it. Think about keeping up your own commitment to yourself first, to others later, and the impact it creates on your belief and your credibility in the eyes of others. Personal branding happens through repeated small acts.

Following is an incident in Bihar state, India. Rukmini Kumari, 22 years old, was pregnant and counting hours for delivery as she entered the examination room. Everyone was looking at her, and having known her condition, invigilators had made all medical arrangements in case she goes into labour while in the hall. She wrote the examination, and that night she got severe labour pain, and the next day morning she delivered the baby. The next day was her science exam. The doctor advised her to rest for a few days and to skip the examination in such a condition as it is not safe for her and the baby. She would not listen. She was bent upon taking the examination and so, the doctor planned to take her to the examination hall in an ambulance.

Everyone in the hall was surprised to see her commitment towards taking the examination. No one would have noticed if she had not taken the examination. She had every reason to skip the examination. Her determination and commitment were very high, and she did not take shelter under the umbrella of excuses. She found a strong reason not to skip. We cannot imagine her mental and physical condition while writing the examination.

Nothing came in her way to achieve what she wanted. Rukmini is an inspiration for others by showcasing her grit, willpower, commitment, and determination.

Success and excuses do not go together. If you opt for excuses, forget success. An excuse is one of the biggest obstacles to achieving something meaningful. Excuses are an easy route to escape accountability. In every situation, you have a choice to do something or not to do with excuses. You are what you choose. Do not start giving excuses, saying the other side of the fence is green. Start watering your side to make it green. Making excuses by blaming the circumstances and people is easy, but it will not take you anywhere. Find one strong reason to do it instead of finding a hundred reasons not to do it. David Schwartz calls excuses a failure disease and says that people cut themselves short and rely on excuses to avoid doing things.

Typical reasons for excuses –
- Not keen to do something
- Not ready to take up responsibilities
- Looking to be in the comfort zone
- Not ready to face the new situation
- To look good to others
- Not willing to take risks
- Caring too much about what others think
- Being impulsive and reactive (unable to focus)
- Not a priority
- Laziness and tiredness
- Syndrome of 'If only....'
- The feeling of being unlucky
- Health issues
- The feeling of not being smart or intelligent

There could be many more. Reflect on your typical excuses and see how this can be replaced by commitment. It is better to accept a mistake rather than make an excuse. Break the habit of finding excuses to enhance your personal productivity. Do not allow excuses to derail your progress. By taking shelter under excuses, you will be driving the success away from you. Be gritty without excuses.

My top three improvement action points

1.

2.

3.

8

DEVELOPING A CHANGE MINDSET

If you change the way you look at things, the things you look at will change

— **Wayne Dyer**

Change is the only constant thing in life and is a beautification process. A caterpillar undergoes many changes to become a butterfly. What emotions come to your mind when you hear the word change? Typically, it invokes a negative emotion and the mind, by nature, resists change and tries to maintain the status quo. The law of nature is to change, and change happens irreversibly.

Look at the words of Brian Cox, a physicist, "We all age as the years pass – people are born, they live and die. Out there in the universe, those grand and epic cycles peer the eternal and unchanging. But that's an illusion. See in the life of the universe, just as in our lives, everything is irreversibly changing." Getting disorder is inherent in nature and it is called entropy. The first mindset to being successful is to accept that change is inevitable and to adapt to the change.

According to Darwin's theory, the species that does not adapt to the change will be extinct in due course.

The same thing is told differently by John Welsch, an American business professional, which is applicable to companies: "If the rate of change inside the company is lower than the rate of change outside, then the company end is coming soon." As we are talking now, change is happening around the world, with or without our knowledge. Keeping ourselves open to sense the signals of change and accepting the change is a must in your personal and professional growth.

Be ready to change proactively before you are forced to change. Do not wait for a situation when there are no options but to change. Winning companies around the world are good at proactive change. As soon as you sense the need for change, prepare your mind to respond to it. To respond to external changes, are you working internally to change? What habits of yours, practices, current skills and capabilities, and behaviours are not conducive to adapting to the changes? You cannot change the happening of uncertainty. You can change your ability to face uncertainty.

"Reality is created by the mind. We can change our reality by changing our minds," said Plato.

Mark Sanborn, leadership speaker and author, has emphasised the speed of change with his words, "Your success in life isn't based on your ability to simply change. It is based on your ability to change faster than your competition, customers, and business."

Do not take for granted that the current situation, however good it is, will prevail forever. Problems, like viruses, will also mutate. Be ready to accept challenges and change.

The mindset that resists change is complacency, cynicism, the belief that old things are good, anything new will have a lot of complications, emotional issues, cultural blocks, too busy to change now, justifying the status quo and resistance to leave the comfort zone. A few expressions are: "Let things go as it is. Why wake up a sleeping lion?" "We already attempted, and it did not work," "Very difficult to change here," and "There is no need to change." The power of change is within yourself. Change starts from the mind, and you cannot change anything without changing your mind first.

There are three types of people who respond to changes. The first category, called laggards, are not able to recognise the value of change and hence do not change. The second category is those who see the value of change but do not try to change. The third category people are winners, who see the value of change and take pain to change. Which category do you belong to?

Develop a mindset with a belief that the same as yesterday is not good enough. Change is an opportunity to test your capability and learn new things. Get yourself motivated for the change and be ready to embrace new situations that change brings in. The surfer knows how to ride on the waves of the sea. Changes will keep coming like sea waves, and you should be like a surfer to ride over them; otherwise, you will find yourself beneath them. Be ready to lose something to get something better.

A golfer finds some challenges with his play. He seeks the help of a professional coach to overcome them. The coach studies his play and says that the problem is with the golfer's hand position and grip while hitting the golf ball. He demonstrates, and the golfer tries—some shots go well and a few not so well. The coach advises him to continue to practice, and he will find comfort with the new grip over the period with a message, "Do not slip back to the old grip." The golfer, over the weekend, starts with a new grip but finds it very uncomfortable. He goes back to the old grip and finds it very comfortable. Although his problem comes back, he thinks it was not the right advice by the coach. Old habits always "feel much better." Don't you see such a phenomenon happening with many people around? Have you experienced this in your own attempt to change, where you slipped back to old habits? We are creatures of habit. We typically reject anything new.

Each day, a bird would shelter in the shaky branches of a tree that stood in the middle of a deserted place. It didn't want to fly to a better place. One day, a whirlwind uprooted the tree, forcing the poor bird to fly to a faraway place, searching for shelter. It landed in a forest full of fruit-laden trees. Remember that calamities and challenges can also be better for you. COVID-19, though deadly, brought in many new perspectives.

The extent of results you get in solving a problem, in growth or any change depends on whether you have a victim or victor mindset. In the victim mindset, you blame external situations and people, and in the victor mindset, you take ownership and work on things you can control.

Develop the will and skill to change. Don't just be interested in talking about change, but be committed to change. Believe strongly that the only way things are going to change for you is when you change. If you need sustained success, be ready to change with time.

My top three improvement action points

1.

2.

3.

9

BE PROACTIVE

The way to bring about change is to be proactive and active

— **Octavia Spencer**

Being proactive means taking responsibility for initiating actions rather than watching what is happening and reacting to it.

See the beautiful words of Stephen Covey, "Look at the word responsibility—'response-ability'—the ability to choose your response. Highly proactive people recognize that responsibility. They do not blame circumstances or conditions for their behaviour. Their behaviour is a product of their own conscious choice, based on values, rather than a product of their conditions, based on feeling."

A reactive person makes decisions based on the circumstances, but a proactive person takes decisions considering alternatives. Reactive behaviour is where action is taken after the incident has happened, and efforts would be minimal. In proactive behaviour, problems are anticipated, and best efforts are made to mitigate them.

Three approaches are used in problem-solving, typically in the technical domain. The first one is a reactive approach, where actions are taken after the incidence of the problem. The second one is preventive, where actions are taken to address known problems to avoid reoccurrence. The third one is a proactive approach. It is about solving potential problems even before this happens. Here, all problems that might happen but not necessarily happen are listed to address to avoid future negative impacts.

To know whether you are proactive or reactive, list all actions initiated by you without someone telling you in the last month. Also, look at those actions imposed on you. Those proactive actions identified by you that align with your goal make you more productive.

I recently visited a company. The person I wanted to meet was busy with customer calls. When I asked him what the urgency was, he said a material that was supposed to be dispatched a few days back was delayed, and the customer is chasing that. The date of dispatch was agreed upon by this person. When I asked him why he did not inform the customer about the delay and the reason why the agreed date/time elapsed, he did not have an answer. He demonstrated reactive behaviour. Had he been proactive, he could have saved customers time and strengthened the relationship as well.

There are three types of people. One will act after a thing has happened or only when it comes to them. Such people do not attempt something unless they see someone else has already done it or is currently doing it. The second type is confused and wondering what is happening. The third category is the proactive ones who make things happen. They are self-starters.

To be successful, you need to be proactive. Look at the following guidelines to support you to be more proactive.

- Remember that you are alone and responsible for your own success. Others can support you in your efforts and initiation of actions to be you. Take responsibility for your actions and

life. You are the producer, director and actor of your film called life. Take ownership of your successes and failures.
- All of us have problems. The one who would focus on solutions and find effective ways to tackle the problem will succeed. Focus on those things that are in your control and initiate actions. Answer these questions while analysing any problem:
  1. What happened?
  2. Why has it happened? What are the root causes?
  3. What can I do about it now?
  4. How can I ensure that the problem will not occur again?

The answer to the fourth question is proactive action towards prevention.

- After setting the goal, work backwards to decide and list the actions you need to initiate and execute to achieve the goal. Be accountable for your actions, and do not blame anyone in case you are not able to achieve the goal. Eliminate unnecessary tasks.
- Believing in luck and waiting for something to happen is a waste of time. It will not take you towards your goal. The more effort you put in, the luckier you will be.
- Take action every day proactively and consistently for the completion of the task you have scheduled.
- The type of people around you may have an influence on you. Be careful and avoid being negative and reactive.
- Do not justify reactive behaviour if a thing does not work out. Be honest and take responsibility to correct and move.
- Before taking on any project or task, do thorough planning at each step, including alternatives if things don't go as per plan, ways to mitigate possible problems or risks on the way, resources needed, etc. Do this exercise proactively, and you will be more productive. Just starting a job without a plan will hamper productivity.

- Take preventive actions. For example, checking the oil level in the car once every three months will reduce the risk of car breakdown later.
- Start doing something which you are passionate about. You will learn to be proactive.
- Resolving to make tomorrow better than today is proactive thinking, rather than just being hopeful, without taking action, that tomorrow will be better.
- If you run an organization, strengthen a weak department, function or people by proactive identification and action.

Proactive people are more productive. They do things without being told and volunteer to take additional responsibility. They take control of the situation and direct old habits in a new direction. Go after problems to solve them proactively. Are you the one?

My top three improvement action points

1.

2.

3.

10

POWER IN QUESTION

The answers are all out there, we just need to ask the right questions
— **Oscar Wilde**

Kaizen is an incremental improvement thinking process mastered by the Japanese. It can be applied in the office, factory, home and at the individual level. One of the ground rules of Kaizen is to question the status quo and not to accept things mechanically as they are. The more questions asked by leaders to their teams, the more improvements are likely to happen.

The soul of great coaching is asking the right and powerful questions instead of answering them. Right questions make you reflect, think, and take action. Apart from asking questions to others about the situation, start asking questions to yourself. Right questions will give deeper insight into the situation, challenges, and ways to address them. For spiritual seekers, "Who am I?" is a beautiful question to ask oneself.

In our schooling, we are trained to answer the questions and not much to ask the questions itself. In an organizational context, with dynamic market changes, we need to prepare more thinkers by posing questions than doers.

The Government of India used to present the annual budget every year on a specific day in February at 5:30 pm Indian time. This practice was going on for more than 60 years after the British left India in 1947. The reason was that this time was convenient for bosses in England, considering the time difference between these two countries. This practice went on for decades without being questioned. In recent years, the subsequent government questioned this age-old practice and shifted the budget presentation to the morning session.

Asking "Why to do?" a task, project, business, or activity before doing gives a powerful insight into the purpose of doing something. This question should precede the questions, "What to do?" and "How to do?" By asking all three questions together, one can move better with the activities. Recently, an Assistant Professor at a university known to me for years wanted my help in looking for a job in the industry. I asked him to meet me in person and started the conversation with him with the following questions to elicit more about his intention. My first question was why he wanted to change his professional life, what issue he has specifically in his current job and what he is expecting in the industry. I found that he was not clear in answering these questions and wanted to change because someone told him there were better opportunities to grow in the industry.

In subsequent discussions, further questions related to what he really wants in life, what he enjoys doing more and how the industry may accept him came up. I told him to reflect deeply for a few days on these questions and revert. Later, he came up with an answer that he had decided to continue in the teaching line and wanted to make an imprint there. He met me seeking answers and went out with questions and found answers by himself. This is the power of asking questions.

The head of the quality of a manufacturing company wanted my help to know how to improve customer orientation by his supervisory staff. In the initial discussions, I asked what exactly customer orientation in their job meant and how this will help them to do a better job and benefit the company. He answered that it will help a lot, but I was not convinced. I asked further what issues they are facing dealing with customers and what triggered him to think of this program. He got better clarity and listed all the issues seen with customers and the negative impacts it created. The next question was what behavioural changes in their day-to-day activities are expected from supervisors after the program. Based on this, it became easy for him to get an answer to his first question.

One concept of 'Why-why' analysis is used in the problem-solving approach in quality. This is meant to identify the root causes of the problem to find a permanent solution to the problem to avoid recurrence. Thinking here is to start with the first question on why the problem occurred. One example may be appropriate. The car stopped suddenly while driving, and 'why-why' questions can be like this:
- *Why did the car stop?*
- The battery stopped working.
- *Why did the battery stop working?*
- It was not getting charged.
- *Why was it not getting charged?*
- The condition of the battery was deteriorating.
- *Why did this happen, and why was it not checked during service?*
- Servicing was not done for a long time.
- *Why was the servicing of the car not done in time?*
- Servicing was not scheduled, and there was no trigger to remind.
- *Why was the scheduling of service not done?*
- It was not considered important.

As you can see in the above example, the root cause is different from the surface cause seen. A permanent solution is possible by addressing the root cause.

Questions have the power to trigger thinking, get clarity, improve and find solutions to problems. Asking questions is one of the competencies and starts with a child's curiosity. Go ahead and start framing your next question.

My top three improvement action points

1.

2.

3.

11

OVERCOME PROCRASTINATION

A day can really slip by when you are deliberately avoiding what you are supposed to do
— **Bill Watterson**

Putting off an important task to a later date regularly and deliberately is called procrastination. It is about putting off till tomorrow what should have been done today. All of you procrastinate at some time or the other. You may tend to do a lower-priority job that gives you more enjoyment, putting off the important ones which may be tough or boring. If it becomes a regular habit, it will affect productivity seriously and may add to the stress. Procrastination has killed more dreams than failures have. To improve the productivity of yourself or your team members, you need to understand the reason for procrastination, the impact of that and the ways to deal with this.

A few possible reasons for procrastination could be:
- Lack of confidence
- The attitude of "let us address when it comes"
- Fear of failure
- To avoid confrontation
- Waiting for a perfect time to start
- Laziness

- Inability to take decisions
- No interest in doing something not enjoyable
- Casual approach
- Lack of priority
- Thinking that delaying may solve the problem
- Not sure of the solution
- Getting distracted easily
- Feeling that solution may spoil the situation
- Does not want to face the solution
- Unpleasant or getting bored doing the task
- Last-minute rush attitude
- Lack of self-esteem and self-control
- Emotional barrier
- Overconfidence
- Lack of capability
- Tendency to do a perfect job
- Looking for the right mood to start

Watch your activities in the last month and identify the tasks postponed and the associated reason why you postponed. How many of the above reasons are applicable to you? If none is applicable, great. Identify the reasons that are coming up often. Attempt now to change your behaviour to avoid postponing.

I was postponing writing this chapter, taking an excuse of no time for myself. When I reflected deeply, the actual reason was something else. It was about disempowering thoughts like "Who will read this?" "Am I good at writing this?" "What is so special when there is enough information outside?" and so on. The real action happened when I started making empowering thoughts like "I share what I know", "someone will get the benefit for sure", and "I have experience in writing".

Procrastination has many negative impacts that will affect productivity. Some of these could be loss of opportunity, loss of time, more effort, penalty, impact on quality, stress, guilt feeling and loss of trust and credibility. In the above exercise, list the impacts of your postponing behaviour.

Have you come across persons who postpone till the last minute of the deadline? They get a rush of energy only at the last minute. Another type of postponement is of items which are open-ended and not driven by deadlines. I met a person a year back who said that he wanted to do an MBA, and he is saying the same thing until today. Non-deadline-driven postponement is more damaging than deadline-driven postponements.

Remember that your behaviour of procrastination is developed over a long period. With this, there is no quick solution which can help you to overcome. By being conscious and through regular practice, the tendency to procrastinate can be reduced. Some of the ways you can attempt are as follows:

- Visualise the benefits, including productivity, you would get by not postponing.
- Split the whole activity into small bites to take up small portions at a time and with a defined frequency.
- Have goals that will motivate you to take action. If goals are important for the organization as well as for you, you tend not to postpone.
- Start the day with the tasks you are likely to postpone and difficult ones.
- Identify your most important tasks to do than the easy and comfortable ones. With this, the tendency to put off uncomfortable tasks will be reduced.
- "There is no right time to do the wrong thing; there is no wrong time to do the right thing." Believe that any time is a good time to start the activity. There is nothing like the right time. The right time is when you decide to take the first action. Start even if you are not fully clear of the path to reach the goal.

Allocate time to think. Making a beginning is a motivation to move further. The journey of a thousand miles begins with a single step, and another and the next one. Stop analysing too much before starting. Push yourself to start.

- People who want everything in a perfect way will have a challenge to start. Do not be a perfectionist. Start small, even imperfectly.
- Celebrate small wins by not postponing to get yourself motivated.
- Admit consequences that came up because of your postponement. Consciously learn from it to avoid repetition.
- Understand that being busy will not give results. Setting the right priority will support reducing the tendency for postponement.
- Make a list of things you postponed in the last year and reflect on taking action. It could be in either personal or professional life.
- Include one interesting aspect while doing an uninteresting job. For example, listen to music while cleaning your car.
- Do not blame others or external factors, or look for an ideal situation to start your activity. Be proactive.
- Fix deadlines for each task, schedule it and follow with discipline.
- Do not wait for the perfect mood to start. When you start, you will get the mood.
- Do not allow yourself to be distracted by routine activities like emails and WhatsApp, which in turn may push off critical activities.
- You may deliberately postpone items which are not of high priority now to a later date.
- Think of positive habits you must develop to reduce the tendency to postpone.
- If delegation helps, start doing this.

- Find an accountability partner who can monitor your behaviour of postponement and give feedback.
- Your progress depends on the choice you make—DAY ONE or ONE DAY
- The advantage of starting soon is that you have time to try a new approach if you fail. By postponing, you may miss this.

Every decision has a consequence. Make a choice: pain of regret due to postponing or pain of discipline.

My top three improvement action points

1.

2.

3.

12

LEARN TO LEARN

Once you stop learning, you start dying
— **Albert Einstein**

In this dynamic world, whether you are an individual, company or institution, it is imperative that there is a need for constant learning. What you learnt many years or decades back may not help you today to face the current challenges. It is important to unlearn and relearn to keep yourself updated and ready for the current situation. When you paint your house after many years, you normally scrape the old paint out before applying new paint for a better finish. Is it not? Removing old paint is unlearning, and applying new paint is relearning.

Unlearning and relearning are comparable to the process that our body follows to live, where millions of cells die everyday, and at the same time, millions of cells are born everyday. Here, death and birth happen simultaneously. Unlearning is like deleting an old file and replacing it with a new file with a better version. Empty your vessels before filling them with cleaner water. To become a better version of yourself, work on dropping, upgrading or changing your beliefs.

William Miller, the proponent of the Values Centred Innovation approach, rightly said that learning is like inhaling and unlearning like exhaling. Learning is not the same as having the skills to do a task. It is about applying those skills to derive the results.

Knowledge is like paint in a Paintbox. It is useless unless it is applied in the right way at the right place.

By developing a few attributes, you can enhance your ability to learn better and faster. A few of them are:

Desire and aspiration – Do you have a strong desire to learn? Without this, not much learning will happen. On a riverbank, a student goes to his teacher and asks what he should do to become a scholar like the teacher. The teacher holds the collar of the student and submerges him in the river water for a few minutes. When the student comes out of the water, the teacher asks the student what his thoughts were while he was in the water. The student says that he was aspiring only to get some air to survive, and nothing else came to his mind. The student got the answer that he must aspire to learn, without distractions, to become a scholar like his teacher.

Dedication and commitment – Having desire alone is not enough unless there is a dedication and commitment to put in the effort to learn. Only inspiration is not enough without adequate perspiration. To learn something, be ready to sacrifice some of the comforts. Interest alone is not enough. Interest is like someone wanting to learn swimming, and commitment is like taking a plunge into the water.

Discover – They say that your Guru will appear when you have desire and dedication. You will find ways to learn with your sincere efforts. With excuses and without struggle, you will not find the right ways to achieve your goal.

Reflect – You learn a lot of things every day by reading books, interacting with people and observing. How much reflection are you doing on these learnings for them to become a part of you through implementation? I have seen people reading a lot of books but not reflecting enough on what is learnt. How much we digest is more important than how much we eat to take care of our body.

Application – Reflections must be implemented to get the real benefit of learning. I read somewhere that you cannot become a good lover by reading a book or seeing a video. A pinch of application is better than tons of abstraction. The real benefit will come only by application. Input is what we gather, and output is what we apply. The output should be higher than the input. It is rightly said that **knowing is not the same as doing** (the author of the book what you are reading has published a book under this title). Only learning without implementation may lead to the illusion of competence.

Share – By sharing and teaching what is learnt through the application, your learning will multiply. It is said that we must learn with the intention of sharing. By this, we will be very serious about learning. It can be through writing as well.

Joseph Joubert rightly said, "To teach is to learn twice over."

Learning is an attitude and one of the most essential life skills as well. Learning is a serious activity. It is costly. It costs your time, energy, focus and attention. It is one of the good investments you make in your life. Learning ends only when you leave this world. It is a lifelong activity, and you learn best when you develop an attitude of always being a student. In Sanskrit, the student is called 'Vidyarthi,' meaning one who seeks knowledge. Behavioural change for the better is a consequence of learning. Otherwise, learning is a waste.

In Zen philosophy, they say, "Before enlightenment, you chop wood and carry water. After enlightenment, you chop wood and carry water." The only difference between before and after is your attitude and demeanour towards the work.

Learning is not compulsory. It is an option you take if you want to be successful in your chosen path. As a mentor, I advise companies to invest money in training and help employees learn. It is expensive for them. No doubt about it, but no training is more expensive to the organization. In the current dynamic market, the job for life is to be replaced by learning for life.

Hector Garcia, in his book *Ikigai,* has elaborated on the benefits of learning: "Our neurons start to age while we are still in our twenties. This process is slowed by intellectual activity, curiosity, and desire to learn. Dealing with new situations, learning something every day, playing games, and interacting with other people seem to be essential anti-aging strategies for the mind."

Like learning by individuals, there is a need for organizations to learn. The only way organizations can learn is through documentation of lessons learnt from failures, experiences gained in changing environments and facing various challenges. Without documentation and deployment appropriately, there could be a risk that learning is lost with people who leave the company.

The brain is like a muscle. When you learn new things, it will get stronger. The more you challenge your brain, the more cells grow in it and the things that are otherwise considered challenging and impossible to overcome become easy.

Every challenge gives an opportunity for lifelong learning (LLE), which is a part of the word Cha**LLE**nge.

Dedicate your time to in-depth learning. When you read a book, listen to a lecture, or attend a training, write your key learnings to reflect on and implement. Shallow learning will not take you high. The more you learn, the more luck will be on your side. To learn more, start teaching what you have learned. What is your learning today? Keep focusing on these learnings to learn better and grow. Happy learning!

My top three improvement action points

1.
2.
3.

13

AVOID MULTITASKING

Multitasking divides your attention and leads to confusion and weakened focus
— **Deepak Chopra**

Multitasking is the ability to do more than one task at a time. It is about working on two or more tasks simultaneously and with quick switching between them. Though on the surface, it looks like multitasking is one of the ways to be more productive, it is not. In multitasking, the mind tries to refocus from one task to another, which is not efficient. Psychological research also has proved this point. We feel that many things are being accomplished simultaneously, but none of the tasks are done well.

I was in a meeting with the director of a company for a discussion on a proposal. The topic was serious in nature. In the middle of the discussion, his secretary came into the room to get signatures on a few cheques. The purchaser came to get approval for a purchase order. The director attended a few calls on his mobile and even answered a few SMS messages, and in between these, he continued our discussion. The quality of our discussion suffered, and we could not conclude properly. When I gathered the courage to point out disturbances in between meetings, he was, in fact, proud that he could do many tasks simultaneously. He was splitting his attention and could not engage fully in any task properly. He could not easily comprehend the payoff in terms of loss of productivity.

Take the example of multitasking by listening to a podcast while driving a car. It looks like a good idea that you could do two things simultaneously. Apart from the safety of driving, you cannot really attentively listen to the podcast. A few other examples could be watching television while typing an email, surfing social media in a meeting and so on.

In a training session on productivity, one exercise is typically done to prove the negative effect of multitasking. The participants will be asked to write down MULTITASKING IS A THIEF and to also write running numbers representing one number for each alphabet, 123456789101112 1314 15 1617181920. Participants will be asked to keep a timer to count how many seconds this exercise took. Then, the participants will be asked to count the seconds it takes to write down M1U2L3T4I5.... In the end, participants will share the difference in timing and experience in doing the first and second exercises. Invariably, the feedback would be that the second exercise took more time, switching led to more mental strain and ended up with a few mistakes as well. You can try this exercise by yourself and see what comes out.

Even on the computer, when many files are open, it will slow down. Our mind cannot pay attention to two or three things at the same time. Attention switches back and forth between the tasks. In this process, energy is lost, which could be saved if a single task is done with focus. Switching between tasks takes more time, imparts stress, causes quality to suffer and leads to more cognitive energy consumption. Multiple channels will clutter your mind. Multitasking is similar to how a person is juggling 4-5 balls in a circus. Except for the one in hand, all others will be in the air.

When you are in a meeting or face-to-face discussion, do not allow disturbance from mobile and others. Keep your mobile in silent mode without vibration. Focus on the discussion with full attention and by actively listening. Try not to deviate from the agenda of the meeting.

Being present with awareness helps to focus on the current task at hand. Be in the present tense, not be tense in the present. Pay attention to what is going on in your body and mind without any judgment. Observe your mind. Mindfulness is about knowing what is happening while it is happening. Be mindful and not mind full. Daily meditation practice will help to focus on a single task or activity.

The Pomerado technique encourages you to focus on a single task scheduled. It is very simple. Keep an alarm for 25 minutes and fully focus on the chosen task without disturbance. Keep your gadgets away from you and do not allow any other type of disturbances. If needed, you can go to a place where distractions are minimal. After 25 minutes, take a break of 5 minutes and continue with another cycle. Break removes the monotony and provides time to get energised quickly, possibly by a few deep breaths. This deep work has a tremendous effect on your productivity. Schedule your tasks suitably to enable you to use this technique.

Batch up your small tasks like email checking, quick phone calls and paperwork together, and schedule a slot to complete all these minor ones so that your mind is free to focus on important and critical activities.

When you start focusing on a single task without multitasking, others in your team will also start following. As a department, it may be a good idea to allot a few hours in the day where everyone concentrates on a single task without disturbing others. Over a period, this becomes a habit among employees and, finally an organizational culture.

Can we hit two birds with one stone? Hit one bird at a time with full attention. You will enjoy what you do and will be more productive. Stop the tendency of multitasking.

My top three improvement action points

1.

2.

3.

14

WORK ON YOUR INTERPERSONAL SKILLS

> Your career success in the workplace today—independent of technical skills—depends on the quality of your people skills
>
> — **Max Messmer**

We, as human beings, are social animals. We cannot live in isolation, and we will always be with people. A lot of time is spent interacting with people such as subordinates, bosses, co-workers, suppliers, customers, friends, relatives and so on. Working on interpersonal skills helps to build better relationships with people to work in a better environment, enhance positive feelings, bring joy, and contribute to improving productivity.

Grid theory talks of 3Rs, namely resources, results and relationships, and finds a linkage between them. As per this theory, resources are required to get results. If resources are made to go through the conduit of a relationship, there will be a huge positive impact on the results. To enhance interdependent systems and processes in a company, Stephen Covey suggests taking the first step of developing interdependent and interpersonal relationships among employees. In a company, working on and enhancing relationships between employees will contribute to enhancing the outcome. Similarly, work on relationships with all stakeholders.

A relationship is built over a period of time. Time and energy must be invested in this. Include the activity of relationship building in your schedules. Apart from formal meetings with subordinates and stakeholders, plan an informal chat to know them deeply, their concerns, aspirations, and constraints, and see how you can contribute to their success. In your personal life, find quality time to be with family members, relatives and friends.

Energy gets exchanged between people in every interaction. When you encounter another person, you have a choice to act as an energy booster or energy drainer. Either you bring positivity by making the person feel good by interacting with you or feel negative when you drain the energy. Be an energy booster to enhance relationships. If you are an energy drainer, if given the choice, people will try to avoid you and start disliking you. Have you heard this: "Some people bring joy wherever they go. Some bring joy whenever they go away?"

Interpersonal skills are about ways to boost this energy. The first step is to accept people as they are and not as you want. When we walk in a forest, we will see trees which are tall, small, thick, thin, wild, weak, and so on. Each tree is different, and we don't have a problem accepting them as they are without any grumbling. Similarly, in a society, we find all sorts of people. Learn to accept them as they are without any judgment. You have control over yourself and not over others.

Remember that people are interested in themselves and not in you. Identify what their needs are and contribute instead of pushing them in your way. By authority, pushing may work a few times, but not always. When you enter a meeting, instead of saying, "I have come," say, "Glad you have come." Each wants to be identified, recognised, and respected.

Admit your mistakes. Do not pretend to be a person who you are not. Be authentic. People can identify your masks easily. Be open with people to accept feedback and criticism. Learn from mistakes and move on.

Pay attention to the small acts of others and appreciate even a small contribution. Be empathetic, showing interest towards them and valuing their opinion. Active listening will support this. A smile can break many barriers and is considered one of the best ornaments on the body. To get extra mileage from people, increase your smiles per hour. Use this often.

The ego could stop you from interacting and connecting with others. The ego is like dust in the eye, which will blur the image. It is a defensive mechanism to protect your identity. By destroying the ego, you will be creating new possibilities to connect with people. Another factor is high attachment to position, designation, or title. Focus on your role than the title and you will be accepted well by others. Replace egoistic words—I, me, my and mine—with "you." Instead of seeing the situation from your world, get into the world of other people to see from their point of view. Remove dust from your eyes.

"The most important single ingredient in the formula for success is knowing how to get along with people," said President Theodore Roosevelt of the US Communicate explicitly with clarity. Honour your commitment. Give constructive feedback instead of criticism, comparison, crying, complaining, condemning, and commenting unnecessarily. Be grateful to people, even for small deeds. Look at the positive side of people instead of finding fault with them. Do not keep on grumbling. This will keep people away. Show care and concern for people.

Work on your personal branding, including the way you express yourself, your dress, your body language, manners, and etiquette. People get connected well.

When you interact with people, try to go empty. When you go with an attitude that you know all and you are superior to others, you are not ready to receive their valuable inputs and feedbacks.

What kind of enthusiasm do you bring to the people around you? This is contagious. When things go wrong, instead of blaming the one who has done wrong, find out what has gone wrong, what lessons you and your team got and how to prevent it from happening again. Working on a relationship in case of failures, obstructions, and conflicts is more important than when everything is fine around. A perfect relationship is not that you never get angry, upset, or irritated with others. It is about how fast you can resolve and bounce back to normal.

In Germany, for every traffic violation, negative points are given depending on the severity, and these points, called rote Punkte (red points), get accumulated over a period and may end up in a revoked driving license. Similarly, every negative experience by another person who interacts with you may register rote Punkte, and, with accumulation, he or she may perceive you differently. The way you are treated is based not on who you are and what you are but on how others perceive you. Do not allow others to mark rote Punkte in their mental register.

Start liking yourself. Without this, you will find it difficult to like and appreciate others. Interpersonal skill development is always work in process, and no one can claim that they have learnt fully, as each person you are dealing with is different and needs a different approach to connect. Similar machines may have one common operating manual, but each person has a different manual. To connect, study their individual manual.

My top three improvement action points

1.

2.

3.

15

LOSE YOUR OLD SCISSORS

A great number of people think they are thinking when they are merely rearranging their prejudices
— **William James**

The world is changing constantly, whether you are aware or not, whether you like it or not. That is the law of nature. Change is the only constant thing.

John Welsch, former chairman of General Electric, was insisting on proactive change by saying, "Change before you have to." To address the challenges arising from a need for change, you must think differently. Our attraction towards the comfort zone comes in the way of change. You cannot change till you decide and commit yourself to the change.

In college, our teacher used to advise us to solve the last 8-10 years' question papers, which will help us in solving problems for upcoming examinations. By this, we were oriented to think in a particular direction. Getting the same or similar problems in our examinations was a matter of luck. There were many occasions when questions were slightly different and tricky and demanded new thinking. The old pattern did not work. In such cases, we struggled with old solutions which did not work to solve current problems. Life is also like this. Many times, we are stuck with old thoughts, prejudices, patterns, and habits that will drive us blindly to follow a fixed path, and we may not try new ways and options. That is why it is said that yesterday's solutions do not solve today's problems. Old experiences are good, but that should not push us to hang on to old ways without looking at more productive ways with better quality, shorter time, convenience and ease.

Companies and even individuals need to be creative and innovative in the competitive world to improve their products, services, and approaches. Creativity and innovativeness in the company are the sum of these attributes of individual employees. In some of the workshops about innovation that I led in different companies, I asked participants to reflect on what could block someone from being more creative and innovative. Many interesting answers used to pop up in the group discussion. A few of them might be relevant here:

- Ghosts of past failures
- Feel threatened by the change
- Averse to risk
- Fear of failure
- Fear of rejection and humiliation
- Striving for consistency – the tendency to be in the comfort zone
- A belief that an old way is good and that we should not risk changing it
- Lack of confidence
- Complacency
- A lot of pride in old techniques
- Emotional blocks
- Cultural blocks
- Why awake a sleeping lion
- No one cares about our new idea

Few or all of these thoughts will stop us from taking new actions and finding better ways. Creative and innovative skills can be nurtured by practice and being open to change. I came across an interesting message on WhatsApp. While thanking the person who sent it in a group for better impact, I have taken the liberty to use that message in first person here.

I like stationery items and many varieties in it. One of them is a pair of old scissors, which I have been using for the last 15+ years. In the case of scissors, I got stuck with only one pair. This was my favourite item to open envelopes, cut papers, cut tablet strips and so on. This item often finds use in one way or another. Though there are many better scissors with good shape and colour in the market, somehow, I was emotionally attached to my old scissors. My belief was old is gold, and why change when something is working well? My wife and children were not successful in getting me to replace the old one.

One day, I did not find my scissors in its usual place. I searched everywhere but could not find it. My wife and daughter also joined me in my search, but with no results. We gave up searching. I was forced to use the scissors of my daughter to cut an envelope. To my surprise, I found that the new scissors had a better grip than the old one; they had an attractive colour, a better shape, and were much sharper. My wife and daughter felt that a good thing happened to me by losing the old scissors. Otherwise, I would not have tried and used the new one.

I started reflecting on why I did not consider the new varieties of scissors earlier. Why was I holding on to the old one all along, and why didn't I try the new one that was already at home? Why did I come to the conclusion that the old one is better than the new one? What was blocking me?

Think over. It is not just our scissors. We get stuck with old mindsets, thoughts, prejudices, and old habits and may keep on justifying them without considering new ideas and options. We are the ones blocking our new ways. Let us use new scissors to cut out things stopping us. Push yourself out of your comfort zone to explore new paths, challenge your own assumptions, question the status quo, postpone judgements, try and be willing to fail, and take responsibility to change yourself. The future belongs to those who are ready to change and adapt. If you are afraid to cross the river, you will miss the beauty on the other side of the river. Gather the courage to change.

It's good that I lost my old scissors. Search your old scissors and lose them.

My top three improvement action points

1.

2.

3.

16
WORK TOWARDS THE GOAL

"If the ladder is not leaning against the right wall, every step that we take just gets us to the wrong place faster"

– Stephen Covey

Chinese philosopher Confucius once said, "A journey of a thousand miles begins with a single step." That is right. It refers to taking a small action and being proactive. But ask yourself this question: in which direction are you taking the step? If you do not have a goal, you will go in any direction and realize later that you ended up in the wrong place. Getting organized, setting priorities, and using time effectively starts with effective goal setting.

As per Tors, time management + goal setting = productivity. This shows the significance of goal setting, apart from time management, to be more productive. Stephen Covey prescribes one of the highly effective habits that starts with the end in mind. Goals give a sense of direction towards success. Setting goals will energize you to take action, and achieving them makes you more confident.

Short-term goals should be linked to long-term goals. The more clarity you have regarding your goals, the better would be your actions to move towards the goal. The goal should be an aspirational one, meaning it should motivate you daily to do something to reach there. Your dreams to do something unique in life should be converted into goals. Dreams are invisible to the eyes. Convert them into goalposts which you can see, work on them, and monitor progress.

Remember the words of Dr. Abdul Kalam on dreams: "Dream is not something that you get when you are sleeping, but it is something that will not allow you to sleep." It is this dream or goal that should motivate you to get up in the morning and make the day productive. Goal brings clarity on what is important for you. Before doing any task, ask yourself a question, "By doing this, will it help me to move towards my short-term and long-term goals set by me?" If the answer is no, think about whether you should do that job.

Your productivity will be enhanced if your goals are defined as SAMBAR. That is—**S**pecific, **A**ligns with a long-term vision, is **M**easurable, **B**rings enthusiasm & excitement, is **A**ttainable, and is **R**elevant within a given time frame.

While fixing your goal, reflect on the words of David Bowie, English singer and songwriter, "If you feel safe in the area that you're working in, you're not working in the right area. Always go a little further into the water than you feel you're capable of being in. Go a little bit out of your depth, and when you don't feel that your feet are quite touching the bottom, you're just about in the right place to do something exciting." Take on a stretched goal, one that cannot be easily achieved. It will force you to think creatively and focus on meticulous execution. If the achievement of a goal is too easy, it will be boring, and if it is overstretched, you will be discouraged and not motivated to take action. The right goal is one that will exploit your abilities fully.

Follow the Goldilocks rule: "Humans experience peak motivation when working on tasks that are on tasks that are right on the edge of current abilities. Not too hard. Not too easy. Just right."

One of my goals after I left the corporate world was to write a book in Kannada language. The moment I decided on this, I started thinking and spent some time each day reading and writing towards that. I started writing small articles and poems in well-known magazines. After a few years, all the published ones were collated, and with additional writing, a book came out under the title *Sanjeevana*. From my experience, when you start, you may not have a hundred percent clarity of where you want to reach, but it gets refined as you progress. When I started writing another book, *Knowing Is Not Same as Doing*, I was not clear about the title, the number of pages, how to publish it and so on. But the direction was clear that I would write this book to convey human values by quoting small stories or incidents from my life. As I progressed, more clarity of goals prevailed.

Before setting a goal, be clear on:

- How many goals do you want to have and can manage? Remember that whoever chases many rabbits catches none.
- Why those goals? Will it motivate you? Do you have or can acquire the abilities required?
- Will you feel pride after achieving those goals?
- Are those goals aligned with your values?
- Are goals integrated to avoid conflicts among themselves?
- Are your short-term goals linked to your long-term goals?
- Will the stated goals excite you to take actions daily when you get up in the morning?
- Are you ready to forego some comfort to achieve your goals?
- How do you know whether you are moving towards the goal?

It works best to be productive if the goals are written down, including the specific actions and reviewed regularly. Also, make yourself clear on your daily actions to do a bit towards your goals.

Have goals in your area of career or business, relationship, finance, health, entertainment, social and personal. All these need to be balanced. Work out a plan to identify weekly, monthly, and yearly goals and act. Commit your goals to a few selective people who will not accept excuses and support, encourage and make you accountable.

If the goal is a big one, you can think of chunking it into smaller bites to address each smaller one. Do not give up easily when you find challenges on the way to reaching your goal. If you are not able to reach a goal despite your best efforts, it is fine. Do not focus on what you lose, but focus on what you gain. Do not lose heart and try again with necessary changes in your approach, taking the lessons from earlier efforts. In the process of working towards goals, more than reaching goals, one of the successes is who you have become during the attempt. After all, success is the progressive realization of one's idea or goals, as per American writer Earl Nightingale.

My top three improvement action points

1.

2.

3.

17

PAST – PRESENT – FUTURE

If you want to fly in the sky, you need to leave the earth. If you want to move forward, you need to let go of the past that drags you down

— Amit Ray

As I am writing this article, the present is becoming a part of the past, and the future is becoming the present. This is the law of nature and is unstoppable. No one can make the time to stand still. In the timeline, there are only three elements – past, present, and future. As someone said rightly, the past is history, and the future is a mystery, and what is available to us and on which we have control is only the present. It is a gift to us, and hence, it is appropriate to call it the 'present.'

The present will become part of history. If our history has to be good, we must take care of the present well. We will have a challenge to use 100% of our present. A portion of this is eaten by memories of the past or anxieties of the future.

Memories of the past can haunt you as ghosts if you entertain them. Unfortunately, the mind gives more space to bad or negative memories of the past compared to good things that have happened in the past. Like the rear-view mirror of a car, the experience of the past can act as an instrument to guide you now as you enter the future. What will happen if you start driving the car, looking only at the rear-view mirror?

Positive experiences of the past can help you when you face an obstacle in the present. Remember your successes earlier and the ways you could overcome the obstacles. This gives you positive energy to move further. Instead of this, if you are thinking only of failures of the past, it drains the current energy, leaving you with no or low confidence to move further.

You cannot go back to the past and correct all your mistakes or failures. Those events have already happened, and you have no control. No amount of brooding or regret can set the past right. Like in a game of chess, you can't undo a move already done. But, you can make the next move better. Your control is only on the present, taking lessons from past experiences and bringing elements of the past to meet future aspirations.

Past experiences, especially negative ones, get stored in your memory as files. Unless you take active steps to erase those files that are not empowering you, they continue to haunt you. Remember and store the lessons from your past mistakes and not the disappointments. Past is a source for reference and leaving and not a place of residence and living. As per psychologists, one way to erase is to write down all the negative or not-so-pleasant things that happened, what results they brought, your actions, including the mistakes, apologies for the people who got hurt and so on. They say emotions can be transferred to paper, leaving you a little lighter in the present.

Many times, you will realise that the decisions you took were right at that point in time, based on the knowledge you had. But they can turn out to be wrong choices in the present moment. Respect your decisions and move further without regret. Nature is not obliged to give positive results for all our decisions and efforts.

When I was doing my master's degree in engineering, in the last semester, I had to complete extra credits for the fulfilment of the course. Since I had other relatively tough subjects, I was looking for a new subject which would be easy to score and completion of credits. One of my friends suggested taking a topic on the foundation of microprocessors. Though in no way related to my Mechanical Engineering stream, I took it for the sake of credits. After a few classes, I realised the mistake I made in selecting this subject. Somehow, I could manage to complete the subject with a 'D' grade, the lowest ever in my educational career. This mistake used to haunt me for many years. One day, as a part of my reflections on the past, I asked myself about the lesson I learnt from the mistake I made. It dawned on me that I should be careful in the future in selecting any domain not aligning with my liking and I should not be carried away by others' words. The valuable lesson I learnt has helped me later to remain on the path where my core strength lies and to make my own decisions. I have no regrets about any of my past mistakes, as they gave me valuable lessons to use in the present.

The past is like a library with many books about your experiences. Go to the library, search for lessons, and come back to the present and apply. Do not stay too long in the library or bring the library to the present. If you dwell too much on the past, your future will be the same as the past. Your history is valuable, and these are stories written by you. Share with others to benefit from your experience, either positive or negative.

In Hindi language, the word 'kal' means tomorrow as well as yesterday. I was thinking that there was a flaw in the language. Later, I realised that there was no flaw, and both meant the same since they are not part of present ('aaj' in Hindi).

Experiment in the present with the experience from the past to meet your future expectations and to create a history that you would be proud to share later with others. The past is your destiny, and the future is a free will which you can create the way you want by acting today. Do not become a prisoner of the past. Tomorrow is just an imagination and focus today to make that imagination a reality. Today is an opportunity to start creating a future irrespective of what happened in the past. Today is the first day for the rest of your life.

My top three improvement action points

1.

2.

3.

18

DO NOT BE A PERFECTIONIST

Perfectionists are their own devil
― **Jack Kirby**

We must strive to do our job well. No doubt about it. To excel in a job and try to be outstanding or above average is healthy and promotes growth. There will always be opportunities to improve the way we execute a job. But being a perfectionist is different. He or she, as a perfectionist, will set painfully high standards for themselves in anything they do, and anything short of perfection is not tolerated. They expect the same thing from their subordinates and others. This will seriously affect the productivity of the person and others. Excellence is about high standards, and perfectionism is about unrealistic standards. Perfection is being 100% flawless in the tasks you undertake. But this is not possible to achieve on a regular basis.

You will find one or more of the following characteristics from a person labelled as a perfectionist:

- Highly detail-oriented and very critical about mistakes. Looks for mistakes or deficiency first.
- Overthinking on the possible outcomes and tasks
- Critical of oneself and others if any mistakes happen.
- There is only a yes or no. Nothing in between.

- Doing everything in the best way, whether it is important or not, without looking at the efforts.
- Even after getting results, mulling over how it could have been done better. A sense of achievement is missing.
- Defensive when they receive criticism.
- High focus on the results rather than on the process. Not starting something unless sure of the results.
- Not open to suggestions as they might lead to imperfection.
- Demanding the same perfection from others, making them stressed.
- Thinks too much before taking up a task as there is a fear of doing an imperfect job, risk-averse.
- Less sensitivity for time. Waiting for the perfect time to start an activity.
- Postponing the start of a task and the tendency to look for perfect situations when everything is available.
- Failure is not accepted easily.
- Keep on tinkering and find it difficult to finish.
- Inability to see a bigger picture as the major focus is on micro aspects.
- Cannot imagine a situation where others may perceive the job not being done in a perfect way.
- Thinking, "I must never make a mistake." This leads to hesitation in taking risks.
- Less productivity. Excess time is spent getting into very fine details.
- Effect on one's health and relationship. Expecting others to do the same standard of work as oneself adds to the stress.
- Tendency to complicate a small issue and to do a fine job and to procrastinate.
- Missing to see the bigger picture. More focus on the leaves and, in the process, may miss seeing the tree. Will stagnate the growth.

- Likely to miss good opportunities, being very choosy in taking up tasks.
- Sometimes considered as a bad fit in the team. If you are too rigid, no one likes to work with you.
- Difficulty in making a decision. Inability to relax.
- Struggle to delegate tasks.

Are you able to relate any points mentioned above to yourself? If yes, for a few or many, time for you to reflect and work on it to improve your productivity.

I knew a bank manager who could be categorised as a perfectionist. He used to go home by 8 or 9 p.m. while others leave at 6 p.m. Being a perfectionist, he would check everything done by subordinates and keep all papers intact, nothing to be left for the next day. With this, he was always stressed, and it affected his health badly.

Too much obsession towards perfection may lead to a neurotic disorder called Obsessive Compulsive Personality Disorder (OCPD). Let us look at the downside of being a perfectionist. Based on this, you can take points for improvements.

Soshin is a concept from Zen Buddhism, meaning beginner's mindset. Don't worry about being perfect or having all the answers before starting. Be open and eager to learn as you go. Many Yoga teachers insist on starting some practice of yoga and working on consistency first and not bothering about perfecting the postures. Over a period, they recommend improving slowly.

Correctness and precision are valued highly at the entry or midlevel management position, not at the senior level, where being a perfectionist may hamper your ability to see the bigger picture and may come in the way of developing people. It will affect interpersonal relationships as well.

Perfectionists impose ideals on themselves, leading to a feeling of inferiority if things do not go perfectly. They impose ideals and high expectations on others as well, which will come in the way of building healthy relationships. Try to drop the identity of a perfectionist, for whom mistakes and failures will be a nightmare. Accept that mistakes and something not going well are fine. With this, the procrastination tendency fades away. A byproduct of trying to be perfect is procrastination.

Keeping productivity in mind, you need to decide on the level of perfection for a task. It is a balancing act and is possible through constant practice. Expecting more from yourself and others to move towards excellence is positive. Even with perfect thinking, you need not wait for 100% clarity. This is something hard to get. So, take up the task at hand. Start, and you will find clarity along the way.

Being a perfectionist can be a blind spot, and you can take the support of others to recognise and find ways to improve. Accept that 'not perfect' is perfectly fine. Nothing is perfect in life. Be comfortable with people who are imperfect.

My top three improvement action points

1.
2.
3.

19

DEVELOP KAIZEN MINDSET

Average one competes with others. Great ones compete with themselves
— Vadim Kotelnikov

What would be your answer if you were asked, "Are you a better person today compared to yesterday?" The next question would be, "How do you say you are better?" If you can answer affirmatively for both, we can say that you have a kaizen mindset. It is said that the largest room in the world is the room for improvement. Is there an endpoint for improvement? Unfortunately, no. This is because opportunities for improvement have only a starting point without an endpoint. Improvement efforts are an attempt to move towards excellence.

Brian Tracy, Canadian-American motivational speaker, said, "Excellence is not a destination. It is a continuous journey that never ends."

Kaizen is a Japanese word meaning 'continuous improvement.' Masaki Imai, a Japanese management consultant, as the father of continuous improvement. Coined the word 'Kaizen'. Kaizen is a combination of two words, 'Kai' and 'Zen.' Kai means to modify or change, and Zen means to make good or better. Both root words in combination as Kaizen means change to be better or to improve.

In the words of Masaki Imai, "Kaizen is a means of continuing improvement in personal life, home, social life and working life without major investments." It is about incremental improvements.

There is a Japanese saying concerning Kaizen: "If a man has not been seen for three days, his friends should take a look at him to see what changes have befallen him." Of course, 'change' here is meant on the positive side.

Taiichi Ohno, an architect of the Toyota Production System, believed strongly in Kaizen thinking and used to say that something is wrong if workers do not look around each day, find things that are tedious and boring, and then rewrite the procedures and even last month's manual must look out of date. His message to employees was that they must continuously look for opportunities to make things better.

Kaizen incorporates three practices, namely, consciously, consistently, and continuously. Improvement here is not by luck but by consciously planning for improvement, consistently practising daily and continuously working to improve further.

In business, it is said that if you are not working to overtake your competition in this highly competitive world, you are creating competition. You must run faster than your competitors to move ahead. Before that, focus on being a better version of yourself or of your business today compared to yesterday.

The power of compounding works very well with improvements. If you can be better by one percent each day for one year, with compounding, you will end up being thirty-seven times better than what you are today. The other way around is, if you become worse by one percent each day, you will reach zero. This principle is explained by James Clear in his book, *Atomic Habits*.

The Kaizen mindset is about looking at the outcome of whatever you are doing and working on incremental improvement of what you do and how you do it based on what you have learned. Maintain the level reached and work consistently to improve further.

If the tree is not growing, then it is dying. Growth and evolution are the laws of nature. You cannot grow if you are not changing. Be open to change by adapting and improving to grow. Maintaining the status quo is a killer for growth. Growth brings its own anxiety and challenges. Accept it and move away from the comfort zone where nothing grows.

The principle of Kaizen is that no improvement is too small, and the best time to start improving is now. This is applicable all the time, in every condition and everywhere. A simple question to reflect on a daily basis is: "What can I improve today?"

Barriers to the Kaizen mindset could be: reluctancy to change my current ways, why disturb and wake up a sleeping lion, I will change only if needed, I tried a long time back and failed, why take up additional improvement activities, nothing will change with me, I don't see the benefit of improvement, it is difficult to change and sustain, I am already comfortable now and so on. The mind might be set in concrete, and unless you break it with a belief that progress and growth are possible only with Kaizen, you will not see results.

While coaching athletes, a high degree of emphasis is given to the starting posture before running. This posture can significantly affect the result, especially in a short race like 100 meter sprint. Likewise, taking the first step, however small, is very important in improvements. You have won fifty percent if you start. Start now and look around and see what first step you can take. You will see the next step after climbing the first step.

Smart work is needed for Kaizen instead of hard work. Develop a mindset of possibility where you will focus on what is possible and what cannot be done. Using a brain is better than using the brawn. Applying a bit of kaizen thinking is better than talking about theory.

Do not wait for perfect conditions and clarity to start. If you have reasonable clarity, you will improve as you progress. If you make a mistake, accept and correct it immediately. Each experiment in Kaizen gives either results or lessons. There is nothing like a failure. In Kaizen thinking, there is no such thing as a dumb question. Keep on questioning the status quo to improve further.

Any initiative towards improvement may take time to get results. A stone may break with the 101st hit. Do you mean that efforts of the first 100 hits were a waste? Many times, growth happening may not be visible. Do not give up and continue with efforts and regular practice. Sustaining improvement or new standards reached is important to get results in a consistent way. Without a structure for this, improvements will roll back.

John Welsch, who took General Electric to heights, admitted that he made many mistakes in hiring and by other instinct decisions. He used to reflect on what went wrong, get more data, listen to others' feedback and figure out how he can be better next time. This is the Kaizen mindset.

You will be happier and more fulfilled if you continuously evaluate and improve yourself instead of evaluating others. What is your improvement initiative for today, tomorrow and this week?

My top three improvement action points

1.

2.

3.

20

ATTITUDE TOWARDS YOUR WORK

Your talent determines what you can do. Your motivation determines how much you're willing to do. Your attitude determines how well you do it.

– Lou Holtz

In 1962, US President John F. Kennedy, visited NASA once. He noticed a toilet cleaner carrying a broom and other cleaning materials. He stopped and asked him, "I am John F Kennedy. What are you doing?". The toilet cleaner responded, "Mr. President, I am helping put a man on the moon." The president was surprised to see how he found meaning in his work and is passionate about doing his work to the best of his ability. You have a choice on how you look at your job—as a means to earn a livelihood, build a career or serve a purpose. The toilet cleaner selected the third choice here.

A large number of people work mechanically. In offices, being lazy, they find ways to complain about the environment, boss, traffic and so on. The same situation is seen even at home by housewives complaining about their neighbours, children, or husbands. They do not realise that the task and job they are engaged in was chosen by them. Their discontent inside is not allowing them to engage hundred percent in their task at hand.

With this, naturally, their productivity comes down. It will have an impact on the organization, home and also their personal growth.

A temple was being built in a place. One person who was involved in the construction was asked as to what he was doing. He said he was laying one brick over the other. The second worker said that he is contributing to building a temple. The third one said that he was building a shelter for God, who, in turn, would give solace to thousands of devotees who would visit the temple. Though all three were engaged in the same work, their attitude decides how each would feel while working and the contribution they make.

Have you heard of the saying, "Thank God, it is Friday?" Those who use this are the ones who are looking at the clock for the work to be over to go home and look forward to weekends to escape from work. What could be the reasons? Don't they like the work they are doing and is it boring? Finding it tough to do the job for want of capability? Is the environment not conducive to doing the job? Does not have enough motivation? Maybe not compensated enough for their work? Whatever may be the issue, you must take control to make the job interesting for you to say, "Thank God, it is Monday." No one can help you better than yourself. To improve productivity, loving your work is very important. If you can get a job that you like, it will keep you motivated and engaged. You are blessed. If you do not get the one you like, then you must start loving the job you got without grumbling. Start thinking of ways to make it interesting for you. If there is a possibility, change the job to get the one you like.

Do not look at each job or task thinking of WIIIFM—what is in it for me. This is a consumption mentality. If you develop a contribution mentality to give more to your job than you take back, many will be ready to support you, and you will grow. In

BNI (Business Network International) forum, each member in each weekly meeting must refer a customer or an opportunity for each of their co-members before asking for a reference for their business. They believe that you get more by giving more.

A man walking in a desert got exhausted and wanted water. After searching over miles of walking in hot sunny weather, he saw a borewell with a provision for hand pumping and a mug filled with clean water. He felt very happy and, without wasting time, bent forward to drink the water in the mug. As he was about to drink, he saw a board next to the mug, "Prime the pump with this water and fill the mug with pumped water." He was in a dilemma. What would happen if he used the water to prime and the pump did not work? Should he risk using the water in the mug for priming and forego immediate gratification of thirst with already-filled water? Should he drink the water from the mug, not bothering about the next traveller? Finally, he decided to use the mug of water for priming. His joy was immense when he saw gushing water from the borewell. He quenched his thirst, filled the mug with water and moved forward. Prime the pump before drinking. Give first before taking. Stop looking at all work from a transaction angle. Start contributing without expecting anything in return, at least in some areas of your life.

John F. Kennedy once said to his citizens, "Ask not what your country has done for you. Ask first what you have done for your country?" Can you apply this when you work for the organization or your business? Add value first to get more value.

I came across a postman whose job was to deliver letters. He loved his job and was seen riding his bicycle, humming songs, smiling, waving at people and, at times, in casual chats with passersby.

With regard to the attitude one has towards work, Martin Luther said, "If a man is called to be street sweeper, he should sweep streets even as Michael Angelo painted, or Beethoven composed music or Shakespeare wrote poetry. He should sweep streets so well that all the hosts of Heaven and Earth will pause to say, "Here lived the great sweeper who did his job well."

All your work and efforts may not go as per your wish and may not give the intended results. That is the law of nature. Be ready to expect unexpected things, but continue doing your best without giving up. As preached in the holy book, Bhagavad Gita, you have no control over the results, but you have control over your actions. Actions with the right attitude will give the right results.

My top three improvement action points

1.

2.

3.

21

LEARN TO SAY 'NO'

It is only by saying NO that you can concentrate on the things that are really important
— Steve Jobs

How often do you say yes to someone or something when you really want to say no? What stops you could be a feeling that others may get offended and feel bad, you want to be seen as a positive person, or you have some hesitation. Culturally, being Asians, many of us have difficulty saying no to someone or something. One of the reasons which I can attribute to, at least in India, is the way we grew up in our families. In a typical Indian family setup, everyone should listen to the head of the family. Saying no is considered disrespectful and non-obedient behaviour. Submissiveness is imbibed from childhood. With this, the mind is conditioned to think saying no is bad.

I had a chance to interact with Japanese people. I realised that they were very good and polite people to deal with. They respect relationships a lot. Sometimes, the difficulty I used to encounter was understanding whether they meant to say yes or no to a particular proposal. I have observed their uneasiness to say no. It used to be not a direct no but a message of no in many other subtle ways, including body language. There is a saying in Japan that there are many ways to say no, and one of them is yes.

In behaviours, there are three types, namely, passive, assertive and aggressive. In aggressive behaviour, 'no' will be expressed harshly. This may hurt the other person and may spoil relationships as well.

If a close friend asks money from you, in an aggressive approach, you may say, "I have been cheated by many people, including friends. I cannot believe people nowadays. How can I believe you?". In the same situation, in a passive approach, even if you do not want to give money, you may say, "I will think it over and revert to you." The right approach would be a middle path, which is being assertive. Here you may say, when you do not want to give money, "You are my good friend. I understand your situation. Financial dealings between us will spoil our relationship. Let us remain as good friends." Here, assertiveness can also be seen as diplomacy.

For us to be more productive, we should learn to say no appropriately. We need to practise our ways of expression. If your boss keeps on giving you too many tasks one after the other, which you find difficult to deal with, instead of bluntly saying, "Not possible to do," you can perhaps say, "Boss, I am fully engaged in the earlier tasks you have given. Shall I stop all those tasks to do the ones you are giving me now? Should this task be of higher priority to take up first?" Here, you are expressing your difficulty and politely saying no. The worst is saying 'yes' when your mind is saying 'no.' This creates stress and will affect your productivity.

Look at the cost of saying yes when you want to say no. Though your agreeableness makes others happy, internally, you will not be happy. It will hurt you, and you cannot prioritize things that are important to you. In extreme cases, you will start thinking you are responsible for others' emotions and change your emotions depending on others. It will be like giving remote control to others to control you. Anger inside you will not allow you to experience life fully, and your growth may fall. You cannot satisfy everyone by saying yes to them.

Steve Jobs rightly said, "If you want everyone to be happy, do not be a leader. Start selling ice cream."

Some tips to say 'No':

- Sometimes, instead of saying no, just smile. It works.
- You have the right to say no. Do not feel guilty, and respect your own decision.
- A clear no is better than saying 'yes' and not doing what you committed to.
- Develop the courage to say no diplomatically and be firm.
- Buy time if needed before saying no.
- Be true to yourself.
- If you say yes, you must really mean it.
- Your refusal may not mean rejection forever. It only means that you are not able to handle or accept it now.
- Practice to be assertive.

When I left the corporate world to be on my own for the rest of my life, I had many opportunities and offers from various companies to work with them on a broad range of topics. The first thing I did was to prepare a list of things which I would not do. This elimination process gave me better clarity to focus only on things I want to do.

I was interacting with a manager of a company to appraise her on the need for coaching their team members, including her. Before I could complete explaining, she interpreted by saying that what I suggested would not help, and she could not find time as she was overloaded with too many activities. She considered coaching as an activity. She said that she had learnt to say 'no' from a book and said no to my proposal even before understanding or listening to what I had in mind. She could have been a little patient to explore more. Saying no in a reactive mode may sometimes lead to missing an opportunity. Be judicious.

You may find it difficult initially to say no, but you can develop it with practice. It sets you free to do the things you feel are important. If you can say 'yes' and your mind also accepts, go ahead with the 'yes'. When someone disturbs you repeatedly early in the morning by phoning, will you be able to say, "Can we agree to fix a slot for our talks when both of us are free?" Learn to say no or give an indication of negation politely when you are not really willing to accept. Nothing is better than doing irrelevant things that are not meaningful to you. Saying no is not a negative quality.

My top three improvement action points

1.

2.

3.

22
DEVELOP GOOD HABITS

We are what we repeatedly do, excellence therefore is a habit and not an act

— Goethe

Our habits decide what type of person we are and our progress in life. A habit is a task or action that we keep repeating. The result depends on whether we repeat good tasks or bad ones. Bad or negative habits lead to bad results. To be productive, we need to look at our habits very carefully, which are an integral part of our daily life. Habits can make or mar us. Habits are acquired behavioural patterns, regularly followed until they have become almost involuntary. It is about any mental or physical activity done consciously or unconsciously so many times that they have become automatic. One person was riding a horse. Someone asked him where he was going. The former told the latter to ask the horse. Habits are like this horse; your success is greatly affected by habits.

I had the habit of looking at WhatsApp too often and kept commenting forwarding many of them. This unproductive habit pervaded me to such an extent that I would be looking at my mobile, often waiting to receive a new message. I had developed a syndrome — fear of missing out (FOMO). Most of the messages were related to politics, comments by people about the system, helplessness by sarcastic remarks on the government, a few jokes, some thoughts and so on. I should say that all were not bad, but the habit of getting disturbed frequently and wasting my time did not justify the benefit I got from new thoughts. This browsing habit used to be, most of the time, during the day till I sleep. One day, I realised the cost of my bad habits. I could not concentrate on anything and noticed a lack in setting priorities and a shortage of time. It took a lot of effort and is still an ongoing endeavour to come out of it fully. I still use WhatsApp, but in a more controlled manner. It is not making me unproductive. The beauty is that it took a very short time to get into the bad habit, but on the other hand, a lot of time was needed to come out of it.

Bad habits are easy to acquire, many times develop by themselves and are difficult to stop, whereas good habits need a lot of conscious effort to imbibe and are easy to leave.

Dr. Abdul Kalam rightly said, "You cannot change your future, but you can change your habits, and surely your habits change your future." Actions that are repeated many times become a habit, and psychologists say that neurons get formed in the brain with repetition.

Stephen R. Covey, author of the book *Seven Habits of Highly Effective People,* says that to develop good habits three things are required: knowledge, skill, and desire. Knowledge is about what to do and why to do it, skill is about how to do it, and desire is a related motivational factor to want to do it. Burning desire to start a positive habit is the starting point, and with this, convert thought to action through commitment. Plan ahead on where, how, how much, when and who can help. To continue till it becomes a part, maintain discipline to keep up with the practice in between ups and downs.

Some important ways to give up bad habits and develop good habits are given here:

- Visualise all the benefits you would get by developing productive habits. It will motivate you. On the power of visualisation, Zig Ziglar said, "If you want to reach a goal, you must see 'the reaching' in your own mind before you actually arrive at the goal."
- Be open to accepting feedback for improving yourself. Remember the words of Ken Blanchard, an American writer, "Feedback is the breakfast of champions."
- Ensure you have the right people around you. They have a great influence in nurturing your bad or good habits. The environment can influence you immensely.
- List down your Akrasia, the Greek word for weakness or loss of command. It is about doing something contrary to what you want to do. For example, you want to get up at 5 am, but you are getting up at 7 am by hitting the snooze button.
- Start with productive habits consciously in a small way and only one or two at a time. It could be like reading for 20 minutes every day. Winning in small acts will give you confidence and motivate you to continue. Developing a good habit takes time, so don't be in a hurry. Looking for immediate gratification is against building good habits. Do not expect your returns to be linearly proportional to your efforts. By doing something again and again, starting in a small way, like a flywheel, it gains momentum.
- Study autobiographies or biographies of successful people or, if possible, meet a few of them to know their good habits and what you can inculcate in your life.
- Replace using the word 'want' with 'need'. For example, instead of saying I want to get up at 5 am, say that I need to get up at 5 am.
- Recognise early challenges like laziness, excuses, taking the path of least resistance and lack of willpower.
- What restrictions can you create to promote a negative or positive habit? For example, the use of small-size plates to eat

less or automatic transfer of your monthly savings to another account, locked in for years, that will force you to save.
- Routines lead to habits. Look at your routines and make changes accordingly.

To make daily exercise a habit, start with less duration and focus on consistency. Once the consistency is reasonably achieved, work on improving the quality of the exercise and duration. Over a period, daily exercise becomes your habit, and you will not have to motivate yourself to exercise. Taking the first step supports enhancing your identity, which is a key ingredient to continue practising, and building habits.

Identify one small good habit that you can practice consciously related to your profession, family, self-development, hobby, finance, and spiritual growth. Monitor your progress and find an accountability partner who can also track your progress. Treat yourself with a reward if you make small progress. The feel-good factor will develop positive habits better.

My top three improvement action points

1.

2.

3.

23

SCHEDULE YOUR TASKS

Scheduling downtime as a part of your routine is hard but worth it, personally, and even professionally
— **Daniel Goleman**

Planning the task alone will not help unless a decision is made as to when to do it. Fixing a time to do the task is called scheduling. In scheduling, depending on the task, you will allot a particular time and duration to complete the task. You need to have discipline that the allotted slot is used only for the task assigned and not eaten away by other things. The power of saying 'no' comes in handy here. You need to be careful in scheduling. The tendency is to underestimate the duration of the task and realise later that the task cannot be completed fully in that allotted time. As per Hofstadter's law, it always takes longer than you expect. Splitting the task to suit the time availability and keeping buffer time becomes useful here.

Have you come across people who say, "I have not had a single minute to think," or "I have to jump from one task to another during the day," or "Every minute, I am disturbed," or "Issues keep coming one after the other" and "I don't know how the day went by?" What could be the issue which is common among these expressions? It is a lack of setting priorities and scheduling.

I met one of the students who was interested to do a short-term training on industrial safety. He talked very enthusiastically about it. When I met him two years later, he was still talking about his interest in the training and his plan. He did not make any effort to list out tasks that needed to be completed for the training and did not schedule his tasks. As a result, his target to do the training remained a wish. It is like someone aiming his rifle at the target but not triggering it. When to trigger is scheduling and triggering is the action.

The difference between a dream and a goal is only in fixing the time frame. Dreams must be converted to goals with a decision and commitment to completing the tasks. Goals can be achieved only when required tasks are scheduled within the time frame.

James McCay said it nicely: "Nothing ever happens in your life unless you create the space for it to happen."

Parkinson's law says that the work expands to fill the time available for its completion, This talks about the benefit of proper scheduling depending on the tasks.

You should schedule the day with such activities that, by doing them, you would go to bed with the pride of having done something substantial. It is a good practice to do scheduling for the day one day before. At the end of the day, reflect on whether you could keep up your schedule during the day and, if there is a gap, how to correct it the next day.

When someone calls me over the phone at random, I will check quickly if the call needs more time and thinking. If yes, instead of answering something for the sake of it, I propose to schedule a time slot for the meeting over the phone or via video. In this way, I can give full attention to actively listen to the other person and have a meaningful and constructive discussion.

Schedule important activities first and other tasks later. For example, learning by reading a book is an important activity and not an urgent one. If you do not schedule a slot in your calendar regularly, this activity will not be done and will continue to get postponed. Do not clutter your schedule with small tasks. List small tasks in your master task list which take less than 10 minutes and allocate time to look at these together. This batching approach saves time.

In the scheduled time, bring clarity on what needs to be accomplished or done. Be realistic about what can be achieved in the scheduled time. In that allotted time, keep your attention on the task without allowing any disturbances. A phone call, WhatsApp or Twitter message, or a mail notification can destroy time in the current schedule and may negatively impact the next task on your schedule.

Consider the time of the day while scheduling to be more productive. Morning hours are good for work related to critical thinking, analysis, problem-solving, reading and so on. Likewise, housekeeping work at home suits your schedule well on Sundays. Schedule, matching to your energy cycle during the day.

Do not miss to schedule 'me-time' during the day or at least once a week. This is purely your thinking time to reflect on what went well and what did not go well in previous days, ways to improve upon now, new areas to explore and planning for short-term and long-term.

If the planned task cannot be completed in the scheduled time, do not leave halfway. Instead, reschedule it.

Keep a few unscheduled slots during the day for emergencies, for doing odd things, for completing shallow work and other things that might crop up and are beyond your control.

Catching up with any random thing that comes up on the way and doing it immediately is unproductive. Decide if the task is to be done and, if yes, schedule a day and time.

Schedule for the month and the week. The schedule for today and tomorrow should be as meticulous as possible, and the schedules for later days can be rough at present and be fine-tuned when it becomes closer.

By scheduling and achieving, psychologically, you feel elevated, and your productivity will increase. Scheduling a task is powerful and simply having a plan alone without scheduling is a waste of time. You can make things happen by scheduling. What is your schedule for today, tomorrow, this week and this month?

My top three improvement action points

1.

2.

3.

24

MASTER THE ART OF DELEGATION

No person will make a great business who wants to do it all himself or get all the credit

– **Andrew Carnegie**

One of the attributes of successful leaders is their ability to delegate and let go. As Peter Drucker, an Austrian-American management consultant, hints an effective manager tries to use not only his or her brain but others as well. Good leaders and managers know how to manage time, resources, and people. Some managers and leaders, in an attempt to do a task perfectly, want to do everything by themselves. Their feeling is that others may not do it the way they would have done. This adds to their stress, and they end up spending more time than needed, affecting their productivity.

One of the secrets of productivity is to get things done by others so that you can concentrate on the core task you are supposed to do in your role. Have you come across managers doing the jobs of their subordinates? Many find it convenient and comfortable to do jobs of subordinates as it would be relatively easier than the ones they are supposed to do or paid for.

Delegation is a technique not only to develop people but also to increase your productivity. It is about assigning the responsibility and authority to other people to carry out a functional task or to make a decision. Giving responsibility and expecting results without giving the needed authority may frustrate others. Through effective delegation, you will get more time to concentrate on your important tasks, increasing your bandwidth and critical activities for which you are responsible and accountable.

I knew the head of cost accountants in a company. He used to verify every entry in ERP (Enterprise Resource Planning, a business management software) done by his subordinates as he would not believe them and was afraid that their mistake would put him in trouble. The result was that he would be fully tired at the end of each day by working late hours. This behaviour added stress to him, affecting his work-life balance. The probable reasons why he was not comfortable delegating tasks to others and doing jobs for which he was not appointed to do could be:

- Tendency to micro-manage
- Slave to details
- The perception that others are not competent
- Takes too much time to train and delegate to others
- Fear of losing control
- Insecurity
- Not trusting subordinates
- Suspicious about the potential wrong intentions of others
- Thinking that nobody can do a better job than oneself
- Does not like others to get credit
- Fear that others' mistakes may affect his image
- The mentality of hoarding the tasks without involving others
- To make oneself indispensable

The result of the above behaviours by managers and leaders will result in poor development of people, no second-line persons, and an increase in stress levels. Organizations will suffer from the risk of high dependency on a few people.

A Chinese proverb would be appropriate here: "Give a man a fish, and you feed him for a day; teach a man to fish, and you feed him for a lifetime." Training people through delegation is one of the value-added activities in the organization. Delegate those tasks and activities which can be done by others and where your attention is not required.

The following points will help to master the art of delegation:

- Identify the right person who has the skill, time, and who is ready to shoulder the responsibility and who will find the job interesting and stimulating.
- Delegate as soon as possible. Doing it at the last minute leads to stress for the delegatee, which may result in mistakes and even resentment.
- People should feel proud to do the job delegated. Do not delegate the unpleasant jobs only.
- Introduce the task with details. Train them if needed. Support initially
- Buy-in the commitment before delegating.
- Have consistent standards. Documenting before the delegation is better.
- Give ample freedom for the subordinates to complete the task.
- Appreciate their efforts and capability.
- Trust them and do not interfere often. Allow them to do work in their own way.
- Follow-up and review are required to ensure that they are on the right path. Here, the purpose should be to support them with feedback and not police them.
- Appreciate their ideas and reward suitably later.
- Allow them to run freely and your job should be to remove obstacles on the way.
- Share information freely.
- Encourage them to take risks and allow them to make mistakes.

Among many of the wastes in the system, not exploiting the potential of people is one. Here, waste means that cost is incurred but without proportionate value contribution in return. By delegating to the right persons, you will be tapping their natural abilities, helping the company to be more productive.

To start delegating, do not look for excuses like difficulty, time consumption, none being as good as you, loss of control, people not trustworthy, thinking to be in your comfort zone and so on. List down all the tasks you are doing currently and identify the unimportant tasks which can be delegated. Start in a small way and with those who have the skill and will to get initial results.

It is worth taking the message from George Patton on the way to delegate: "Never tell people how to do things. Tell them what to do, and they will surprise you with their ingenuity."

While you work on a delegation to increase your bandwidth, also watch out for upward delegation happening from the subordinates reporting to you. Many times, they tend to do it to escape from accountability, to make their challenge of decision-making easier or to get more time. Consciously handle this to avoid doing a job which your subordinates are supposed to do.

To master the art of delegation, work on sharpening your skills such as listening, empathy, setting the right priority, result orientation, planning, interpersonal skills, effective communication, relationship building, effective review and being comfortable with letting go. Enjoy doing what is important for you by delegating other things.

My top three improvement action points

1.

2.

3.

25

LEARN THE POWER OF FOCUS

The successful warrior is the average man, with laser-like focus

– Bruce Lee

The lack of focus is one of the reasons why people do not get what they want. If you want to achieve something, focusing on it is a must. Focus is one of the secrets of productivity. I have seen start-ups starting with great enthusiasm but deteriorating over a period, predominantly attributed to dilution of focus. If you are focused, you are conscious of your time and you will face any setbacks that come up along the way.

Focus means single-mindedly concentrating on the job, without allowing disturbances. There is a story in Mahabharata. Arjuna's teacher wanted to test the level of focus of his disciplines and give them a test. He shows them a bird sitting on a tree and asks each one of them to explain what they see before shooting. One student says that he sees a tree, the second one says a bird and so on. When it comes to the turn of Arjuna, he says that he sees the eyes of the bird and nothing else. That is the focus.

Focus can be achieved through practice. When you have decided to do a task and say you have allotted 30 minutes, in this period fully focus on what you are doing and do not allow any disturbances like phone calls, emails and so on. You will achieve more. By nature, the mind wanders to go to the past and future, and drift to other things in present. By practicing consistently, you can provide hundred percent attention to a single task.

As a mentor, I have had many opportunities to guide industries on various development fronts. My initial question is about what they want to focus on in the upcoming months of the year. After a few discussions, we will arrive at the top 3-4 areas or goals that need focus to move further. The challenge would be to ensure they stay on that month-on-month to get some results in the area. I am convinced that if all employees are trained to align and focus consistently on the top few areas identified, there will be substantial improvements.

As an individual, ask yourself this question. What areas do I want to improve or focus on in the next few months, and how will I ensure that I remain focused in these areas every day until results are seen?

An employee complained to his boss saying that he had a lot of disturbance from his colleagues due to their chats, calls and so on. He was not able to concentrate on what he was doing. The boss asked the employee to take a glass of water, fill it up to the brim, and walk with it around the office. The only condition is that he should not let any water spill. The employee walked carefully and was successful. Now, the boss asks him whether he heard the noise of his colleagues while walking. The employee said that he did not as his mind was fully focused on the glass to avoid spilling. He learnt that he would not notice any disturbance if he was truly focussed.

I had an injury in my right knee joint a few years ago. The operation was done by a renowned orthopaedic surgeon. He had done hundreds of operations at ease and gave me a lot of confidence to help me recover faster. I noticed a secret to his success. In the operation theatre, he used to come only for 15-20 minutes to give a final touch. All pre-operation and post-operation work was done by other doctors. Through his focus, the surgeon mastered the art. Since he is good at his job now, he can do his work without wasting time and effort on other mundane things which can be done by others.

Daily practice of *Dharana* as taught in yoga helps in the increase of focus. In this daily exercise, you will practice focusing on your breath or a sound with closed eyes.

In my trainings, I give an exercise to participants to make them understand the importance of focus. I ask them to see things around them in the room and write down all items with round shapes. The list usually comes out well. Then, I ask them how many objects were square or rectangular in shape. The answer invariably is zero or a few, even though there were plenty in the room. Since their focus was only on identifying circular objects, they did not see the other shapes, and the mind did not register them.

Here are some ways to help you focus on your tasks:

- Unplug all your disturbances like mobile phones, internet and so on during the period.
- Prepare your mind before the task and calm down.
- Prepare a schedule and reasonably estimate the time needed for the task well in advance.
- Sometimes, background music helps focus better.
- Breaks in between the tasks help to focus better. Deactivating and reactivating allow you to stay focused.
- Doodling and writing improve the focus on what is being done.
- Be organised so that other things do not distract you. Get rid of a cluttered schedule.
- Practice meditation and exercise regularly.

- As per the Journal of Nutrition 2012, the study has shown that focus can be increased by hydrating oneself. So, drink a lot of water.
- Avoid multitasking.
- Identify the areas you want to improve and stay focused on those areas.

One who is after many rabbits will catch none. What you focus on expands. If you focus on problems, that will grow. Similarly, solution space also grows if you focus on it. Identify areas you want to focus on to make them grow.

My top three improvement action points

1.
2.
3.

26

WORK ON YOUR HEALTH TO BE PRODUCTIVE

All work and no play don't make Jill and Jack dull, it kills the potential of discovery, mastery, and openness to change and flexibility and it hinders innovation and invention

– **Joline Godfrey**

In the pursuit of being more productive, there might be a tendency for you to work continuously without relaxing in between. Anything in excess is bad including obsession to be more productive. In extreme cases, it may lead to a sort of stress ending up in health issues and premature ageing. It would be like someone driving on the highway without pausing to fill up fuel for the vehicle. They say, "Pause to look at the roses," meaning that while walking, pause a bit to see the beauty of roses, their colour, fragrance, and shape. The pause gives rest and relaxation to the mind to take up further walking more productively. In the busy world you are, taking a pause is one of the good habits you need to develop.

Working too much can be bad for you. Workaholics have higher chances of getting into depression, loss of memory power, difficulty in learning, loss of sleep, loss of appetite, strain on relationships, impact on performance and so on. All these will have an impact on the overall mental and physical well-being. Many times, you are more productive when you do nothing.

To be more productive, apart from work, it is a must to take care of the health of body, mind, emotions, social aspects, and spirituality.

Physical Health

Swami Vivekananda used to say that playing football is as important as reading the Bhagavad Gita. A healthy mind stays in a healthy body. One with physical illness cannot think and focus well and gets disturbed by the body, often leading to lower productivity.

Physical health means no uneasiness or pain in the body and is not about the absence of disease. See how your energy can be at a high level throughout the day. Develop daily routines and habits to eat nutritious food, do regular exercises and yoga, consume enough water, take care of personal hygiene, take intermittent breaks to rest and relax, restrict consumption of alcohol and cigarettes, and allocate enough time for sleep. If you don't find time for health, you are forced to keep time for ill health. Our body is like a temple that protects the spirit inside. Do not neglect to take care of this temple. If you fall sick, remember you are causing pain to your loved ones. Undergo regular health check-ups. Prevention is better than cure.

You may be pre-disposed to some health-related conditions which are genetic. Remember those are not predestined, and you can work on them by self-awareness and taking appropriate action. For example, gaining weight is pre-disposed but not pre-destined.

Keeping your body fit and healthy will boost your self-confidence and self-esteem and support your personal branding. Exercise is a pill that can ease anxiety, improve focus, sleep better, and enhance self-esteem without any side effects. Yoga teachers say that motion is lotion for the body. Do not neglect the body, a fundamental instrument of ours, and nurture it proactively. Nothing can be achieved without the health of the body.

Mental Health

Clear reflections cannot be seen in disturbed water. Similarly, agitated and disturbed minds cannot find the right directions or solutions. Taking care of your mental health consciously is a must for your success. A calm mind can initiate brilliant actions. Signs of good mental health are the ability to focus, calmness, lack of agitation, being alert, sharp and aware, and not wavering or drifting. With regular self-reflection, you can assess the state of your mental health and how it is affecting your productivity.

In my physical training, I asked participants to raise their hands whoever is present in the class. While everyone raised their hands, I am sure they did it with a doubt about why I am asking such an obvious question. My next question was how many of them were present there mentally. Varied answers came. A few confessed that they were thinking about yesterday's discussion with their boss, a few were thinking about the products that were to be despatched tomorrow, and so on. Then I said that their time in training can be productive only if they keep their mind in the present without allowing it to drift to the past or future. The mind, by nature, invariably wanders towards things which are not pleasant which will affect our current feelings which in turn influences our actions. Regularly practising mindfulness, yoga and meditation will help to calm down the agitated mind and keep it in the present moment.

Spend quality time with the family in the evenings and weekends, and do not bring office-related work back home unless it is an emergency. Make it compulsory to have short vacations with the family, say every three months, without taking along work-related issues. You will be energised to do more on your return.

Other ways to improve mental health are having quality sleep, spending time with nature, reducing stress, looking after physical health and relaxing by doing things you like most. Connect with positive people.

Spiritual health

Spirituality may not be able to cure you, but it can support you to cope with your difficulties, pains, and challenges. With spiritual health, you can find comfort in the hardest time of your life and experience life fully. You would have seen people who believe that the body is different from the spirit, that pain is only for the body and who endure physical health challenges with ease.

Spirituality is like the roots of a tree not seen by others. Work on strengthening this invisible force to get visible results. Try to find a meaning for the bigger purpose of your life and with this, you can navigate the ups and downs on the way well.

Count your blessings. Be grateful for things that happened, remember and thank all those who supported you. Accept things that have not happened well and see what control you can exercise in the future. If it is a thing beyond your control, accept it graciously.

Fall in love with taking care of yourself mentally, emotionally, physically, and spiritually. When these things are taken care of, the things that you really want will fall into place. Find meaning in the saying, "All work and no play makes Jack a dull boy."

My top three improvement action points

1.

2.

3.

27

YOUR DAILY REFLECTIONS

Time spent in self-reflection is never wasted – it is an intimate date with yourself
— Dr. Paul TP Wong

Daily reflections are about saying how the day went by without any judgements. It is much deeper and more intense. By deliberate practice of this simple yet powerful technique, you can start creating a better way for tomorrow. Daily reflections are about making yourself aware of what you are thinking, feeling, and doing during the course of the day. Is this the way you wanted your day to be? Daily reflections have a positive impact on the mindset and a time to bring to the surface emotions you underwent.

To make reflections a daily practice, a few steps are suggested. You should commit to a time and duration of the day. If possible, follow the same schedule every day. It could be the end of the day before sleeping or could be the end of your working hours. Decide on the duration, which can start from 15 minutes. Schedule a daily slot in your calendar. To get the best results, consistency is the key. Over a period, it becomes a habit and part of life.

Writing down notes as you reflect on your thoughts, feelings, and results is a good practice. This practice is called reflective journaling. You can try taking digital notes as well for this. What did you do during the day, what went well, what could you not do, and what did you not do are some things that can be included. Write down the positive and negative emotions you felt during the day. Write down more facts and be specific. Examples: "I attended a customer meeting 10 minutes late," "I got up at 6 am, even though I had set my alarm at 5.30 am," "As I started late from home, I drove fast to be on time to the office."

Do not make any judgments and justifications, especially about the things that did not go well. Just acknowledge and accept them and reflect on what you can do to make it better the next day. Do not self-criticise like, "Something is wrong with me", "Why should this happen only to me?" or "I am not good enough to follow the discipline." Negative self-talk is a killer of productivity.

Daily reflections can be made more powerful through a set of daily questions to yourself. Questions trigger thinking, feeling, actions and, finally, results. World-recognised executive coach Marshall Goldsmith is a strong proponent of daily reflections through a set of questions. I have included a few questions here for you to think over. Make changes as required that suit you and start practising. A few questions suited for working employees are listed below:

1. Did I learn one new thing today?
2. Was I punctual and disciplined today?
3. Did I appreciate or compliment one person today for a job done well or who helped me?
4. Have I given constructive feedback to my subordinates to improve?
5. Do I have a clear plan for tomorrow, including the schedule for important and priority tasks?

6. Have I taken a small action today to reduce non-value-added activity or things I should stop doing or am not supposed to do?
7. What positive things happened today for which I am grateful?
8. Have I done something today that will contribute to the increase in satisfaction by my immediate or end customer?
9. Did I complete the tasks I scheduled yesterday fully? If not, what are the reasons? Did I use my time effectively today?
10. Did I spend some time today as 'Me time' to think about the challenges I am facing, my plan for next week and other critical points?
11. Did I discuss today with my subordinates on important topics?
12. What efforts did I put in today to enhance my relationship with others?
13. Am I moving in the direction of the goal set by me? If not, what is stopping me?
14. What feedback did I get to work on further?
15. Did I spend time relaxing, exercising and doing other things that will contribute to my health?
16. Am I finding time to do things I am passionate about?

You can add other questions as needed. Though it is ideal to reflect on these questions daily, if there is a constraint to do so, you can do it once in a few days as well. Writing down your thoughts and insights after going through these questions gives you the opportunity to develop yourself and grow. Use the insights to include actions or areas to work on in the coming days or weeks.

Daily reflections are opportunities to look at daily practices, including adding new ones to increase your competence in a specific area. Regular practice is linked to an increase in your competency. It is a close-looped activity.

Peter Drucker, an Austrian-American management consultant, said about the power of reflection, "Follow effective action with quiet reflection. With quiet reflection will come even more effective action."

Reflection is a powerful practice for enhancing your awareness, conscious living and finding answers for yourself. It is a self-coaching process. Asking repeated questions and regular monitoring prompts you to sustain and improve. My daily walking is sustained and improved over a period, just by fixing a target for the number of steps I must take daily and monitoring my progress. My walking quality has also improved through reflection. It will work for you if you start with a simple question, "How effective was my day? What is it that I should do to get a score of 10 out of 10?"

My top three improvement action points

1.

2.

3.

28

EXPRESS GRATITUDE

Be thankful for what you have; you will end up having more. If you concentrate on what you don't have, you will never, ever have enough

— **Oprah Winfrey**

Have you come across people who talk at length about their success and the path they have travelled to reach the position where they are now, without acknowledging all those who helped them and circumstances that favoured their journey? I happened to attend an alumnus meeting of my friend with their old classmates. He wanted to introduce them to me. In that formal function, one of the persons had become a managing director of a company. When it was his turn to speak, he boasted about his achievements, the qualifications he had acquired and his high-level contacts. There was not a single word about the college, the teachers in the college, those who moulded his thoughts in earlier education, those who inspired him, the environment of college, his parents, friends, and others. He expressed as though credit for all his success should go to him alone. He demonstrated a poor attitude towards gratitude.

When you take shelter under the shadow of a grown tree, will you thank all those persons whom you might not even know and the beautiful nature responsible for growing the tree? When you express gratitude, happy hormones dopamine and serotonin are released in your body that make you feel good, and the immediate beneficiary is yourself. Expression of gratitude, as per psychologists, contributes to positive physical and mental health. Each one of us is like a piece of fabric. A fabric is made of different yarns of thread. These different yarns are like the many people who helped us become a fabric, the people we are today. Let us be grateful to them.

Gratitude is an emotion and a virtue. It is a sense of being thankful and feeling positive for all the benefits and favours received. It is about acknowledging all the things and situations you already have. Being grateful will shift your energy and you will start feeling better. Are you grateful that you can wake up healthy? Are you thankful you have a job or a house and so on? Millions of people are aspiring to be in the position you are in.

William Penn, an English writer, said, "The secret of happiness is to count blessings while others are busy adding up troubles." Aspiring for better things is not bad. But first, acknowledge where you are now and enjoy things that you already have. Happiness depends on whether you focus on what you have or on what is missing.

Gratitude can be enhanced by awareness and practice. At the end of the day, reflect on positive things that happened that day and be thankful mentally for the people who made it happen, the situations that turned out in your favour and the blessings of the universal forces. Express gratitude verbally, non-verbally or in writing, to those from whom you got help or benefit. Do not forget the boatman who helped you cross the river. By writing a gratitude journal, you can feel more positive emotions, increase your self-esteem, relish good experiences and support to build good relationships. Writing down gratitude before you sleep enables you to clear your mind from worries and concerns helps to increase quality of sleep.

Steve Jobs, co-founder and CEO of Apple Inc., expressed gratitude to all those who are responsible for his well-being by writing an email to himself. In his words, "I grow little of the food I eat, and of the little I do grow I did not breed or perfect the seeds. I do not make any of my own clothing. I speak a language I did not invent or refine. I did not discover the mathematics I use. I am protected by freedoms and laws I did not conceive of or legislate, and do not enforce or adjudicate. I am moved by music I did not create myself. When I needed medical attention, I was helpless to help myself survive. I did not invent the transistor, the microprocessor, object-oriented programming, or most of the technology I work with. I love and admire my species, living and dead, and am totally dependent on them for my life and well-being."

Many pray to God daily seeking his favour and blessings to provide things that they wish for. It could be position, money, power, or ability. Prayers are meant not to seek as beggars, but to offer thanks and gratitude to Him for all the blessings and things provided so far.

The one daily routine that has helped me to be more productive over the years is **SAVE**. I start the day with a few minutes of **S**ilence, **A**ffirmations of positive things, **V**isualizing the events of the day as if it is happening and **E**xpression of gratitude. In gratitude, I thank the universal power for bestowing on me health, knowledge, peace and prosperity; my parents, relatives, friends, customers, teachers, mentors, authors, doctors and all others who have helped and are helping me; all animals, worms, germs, bacteria and viruses contributing to me for my existence; the whole universe with earth, moon, galaxy, forest, earth, air, light, water, cloud and so on; and all those like farmers, helpers, soil, seed, manure, air, light, water and worms responsible for providing me with food to survive. This practice enables me to navigate through the day more positively.

The highest level of gratitude and humbleness is thinking, "My success is not because of me, but the efforts and blessings of a higher power through me." Gratitude invites happiness. To whom and what will you be grateful for today? In the ecstasy of current success, do not forget the road you have travelled and all those who supported you to reach here. Have fully what you already have, with gratitude, before looking at new haves. Be thankful for where you have reached in life. Also be ready to face people who will be ungrateful to you. I thank all those who inspired me to write this chapter and those reading it.

My top three improvement action points

1.

2.

3.

29

FACE FEAR AND ANXIETY

Each of us must confront our own fears and must come face to face with them. How we handle our fears will determine where we go with the rest of our lives. To experience adventure or to be limited by the fear of it."

— **Judy Blume**

You may be wondering about the link between fear, anxiety, and productivity. There is one. Fear is common among everyone and is one of the most powerful emotions. It has a strong effect on the mind and body. Some amount of fear will boost productivity. If someone says that he or she does not have any fear, then he/she must be lying. The degree may vary from person to person. In fact, many of our actions are out of fear. For example, someone who tries to save a lot may have a fear that one day, he may be left with no money and may suffer. Here, I am not talking of phobias such as being afraid of snakes, darkness and so on. The fear referred to here is psychological and emotional. A few examples, are facing the audience, contacting a new customer, taking two weeks of break, asking the boss for leave, saying 'I love you' to a girlfriend, fear of losing a job, fear of falling ill and so on. Anxiety is a type of fear that comes from thinking of the prospect of something going wrong rather than what is happening right now. Fear of failure is a king of fears and has a serious impact on the current task you are engaged in and, hence, on the results. Fear can also make you avoid or procrastinate specific tasks. Fear pushes you to remain in your comfort zone, in which growth will not happen.

I know a brilliant student who is pursuing engineering. He has a fear that he may not get a job after the completion of his degree. The news of unemployment, someone failing in the interview and competition makes him anxious. The reason for this fear could be high expectations from parents, no belief in his own strength, previous experiences, childhood trauma or failures, competition or ignorance. Because of this, he is lazy, cannot mingle with others, is not able to concentrate, has difficulty sleeping, lacks confidence and is facing health-related issues. Overall, this situation is seriously affecting his current studies and makes him less productive. He is bringing future problems into the present and suffering.

The fear you haven't faced will become your limitation. Saint Kabir said, "Those who searched by diving deep into seawater, found the treasure. Those who foolishly feared drowning remained on the water."

To increase productivity, you must overcome fear and anxiety. The following points are worth reflecting and acting on:

- Understand that fear is there with everyone, and you are not an exception. Successful people acknowledge and experience it, judging it as positive or negative and take it along.
- Be crystal clear on what makes you anxious and afraid. Acknowledge them and do not try to pretend as if you do not have one. List down your fears of doing something or being in a situation, that is stopping you from acting.
- Realise that fear is imaginary and may not happen. See this acronym of FEAR—**F**antasized **E**xperiences **A**ppearing **R**eal.
- Be clear that your present is because of past actions and in the same way, your future is based on what you do in the present.

If you don't act today, fearing failure, rejection, criticism, and validation, you are losing an opportunity to create a future.
- Read motivational books and autobiographies to get inspiration and take action.
- Think of the worst thing that can happen and be prepared for it.
- Prayer, breathing, meditation and yoga help in overcoming, to some extent, fear and anxiety.
- Reflect on if you are avoiding fear to be in your comfort zone. You cannot grow while remaining in your comfort zone. To grow, be ready to be uncomfortable.
- Do not hesitate to seek professional help if needed.
- Start doing things that scare you. You will get used to it. For example, if you fear talking to a new person, meet a stranger every week to overcome the fear.
- Give yourself an auto-suggestion daily: I am capable of overcoming fear, nothing stops me, I am confident, I am the winner and so on. Affirmations have a positive impact on your life. Avoid toxic words that imply fear and failure, such as, "It is difficult," "I am not capable of handling this," "I can't," and so on.
- Fear happens only in the mind. Condition your mind with the right and positive thoughts. Bravery is not the absence of fear but facing it boldly to move forward.
- To overcome the fear of failure, prepare to accept that failure is not negative and are steps for success. There is nothing like failure but only feedback. No gain without pain. Every failure is associated with a positive lesson. When you fail, think that your attempts have failed, and you are not a failure.

Do not let fear and anxiety stop you from doing your best. Anxiety takes away a lot of cognitive energy and will slow you down. Can you do mental work during airline turbulence? A calm mind is conducive to better focus, engagement, and productivity. The more you focus on positive things, the less your mind wanders towards negative aspects. Convert fear to your advantage. Success is always linked to efforts. Do your best and leave the rest. Worry about the chances you will miss by not trying than worrying about failures. 'Face fear, it GOES. Avoid fear, it GROWS,' said Mahatria, spiritual leader. The choice is yours.

My top three improvement action points

1.
2.
3.

30

MY TEN PERSONAL PRODUCTIVITY PRACTICES

Small deeds done are better than great deeds planned
— **Peter Marshall**

No one can be a master in an absolute sense. I am not an expert to claim that some of the personal productivity practices which I am practising are the best. But still, I want to share a few which have given me tremendous results over a period. You may try if this works for you. Each one of us is different. Any practice must be tailored to suit us.

1. One of my yearly activities is to purchase a yearly planning calendar book. None of my activity which demands a certain time is done without finding an entry in this calendar. In the calendar, I write my schedules in pencil, and once completed, I write over that in pen. This gives me a reminder that the future can be changed, and nothing can be done in past. As I look at this calendar each day, I can see how I have spent the day and week and how fast the time is moving. This book is a part of my baggage wherever I go.
2. Payments towards credit cards, mobile charges, internet, electricity, taxes, and many others are done in time. I don't remember a single case where I had to pay a fine for a

delay or a reminder for not paying in time. The secret is that I keep a few days earlier buffer and do not go up to the last minute. Marking in the calendar is very supportive of this. I believe that doing the thing at the right time saves time instead of attending to reminders, including possible fines.

3. I carry a pen and a small notebook that fits in my shirt pocket wherever I go. I make note of anything I learn by observing, something to explore more, some insights I get, any ideas that occur to me and so on. Sometimes, I use mobile notes. I look at these regularly and decide whether to schedule if it is actionable, dump it if unnecessary or note it in a book if it is a learning point or one to be relooked in the future as a reference. This has helped me to keep my mind free. Many of my training contents have matured over a period from this practice.

4. If someone calls me looking for some advice, tips, or guidance, instead of giving some input on the call quickly, I suggest scheduling a slot for a phone or video conversation or a physical meeting if feasible. My belief is that to give full attention, I must be involved actively. By this, I feel that I can give him/her better value. Before the meeting, I make mental notes on things I may say or ask.

5. Typically, my day starts at 5:00 am. After a few minutes of prayer and affirmations and drinking some black coffee, the next hour is my reading and writing time. I would know the previous day itself, what I would read or write the next day. I must update myself as a corporate trainer and mentor. I have realised that I must vibrate at a higher frequency to guide others. Each of my reading and writing is motivating me to do better. After this slot, I practice yoga for 45 minutes.

6. I am a strong believer in splitting a bigger task into smaller pieces and scheduling the smaller ones. I practice this regularly. This book was not written in just a few days.

When I started, I was not clear about what chapters would come, though I had clarity at a macro level. When I decided to write around 500 words per day or 1 hour per day, more clarity about the next steps came up.

7. All my relatives know that I can be disturbed only after 6 pm for personal calls. I have hinted at this politely in earlier calls. I seldom call or take personal calls in the morning unless it is an emergency. Initially, a few people thought that I was a rigid person, but slowly, they realised the importance of why I try to keep a slot. This has helped me to avoid disturbances when I am doing something.
8. From my college days till today, I wash my clothes by hand. Though there is a washing machine to do this, this small work gives me pleasure that I did it. This small routine practice has helped me to identify myself as a person with discipline and I take responsibility for my work. I have learnt that the way one does small work influences one to do bigger work.
9. One of the annual schedules I practice is to look at all my finances to decide on changes and updates, medical check-ups, insurances, housekeeping of old papers and other things at home to throw all junk not used, dispose of books not needed and so on. This has helped me to keep updated and as I spill out of this, many other important activities over months get scheduled.
10. Time with family as a vacation is an energising event, and I always look forward to it. Over the years, I have been able to do it two times a year, though, for a few years, it is only once a year. Family time has always helped me to bond better with each family member and is a great energy booster for relaxation.

I am happy if any of these practices have given you valuable insights and inspired you to reflect on your life.

What is working for me may or may not work for you. The idea is to share some of my personal productivity practices, for you to reflect on. Having said this, there is a big list of items I am working on to start, sustain and improve. Learning never ends.

My top three improvement action points

1.

2.

3.

31

BE ORGANIZED

> *For every minute spent organizing, an hour is earned*
> *– Benjamin Franklin*

Time is the most valuable asset which cannot be recovered once it is lost. In not being organised, you will waste a lot of time and energy leading to loss of productivity. Remember the instances where you had to search for a long time to trace your vehicle keys in the house, an important paper of a customer in the office, your child's birth certificate and something similar? The root cause of all these is being casual and not organised. Being organized is not a one-time exercise but it should be practiced in a sustained way to make this a habit and a way of life.

Organising may mean bringing chaotic, messy, and disorganised things to a structure. For example, forming a group in the organization to execute a project. It will also mean keeping information or ideas in such a way one should be able to trace them quickly whenever required. Cluttering of things in the house or in the office may lead to loss of time in locating a thing, affect the visual look, and, in some cases, may compromise the safety.

The myth is that being organised takes time and effort. It is not so compared to the benefit of being organised. There is a saying, "The pain of discipline is lesser than the pain of regret later." Being organised helps to relax, to be more confident and, in the end, helps in the reduction of stress. A person who is organized will be able to take up more responsibilities and achieve more in life.

In the Japanese manufacturing system, there is a concept developed for housekeeping called 5S. It is a five-stage process to make the workplace more organised and orderly. 5S in English stands for **Sort out** (throwing out all unwanted things), **Set in order** (a place for everything and everything has a place), **Shine** (keeping area shining by cleaning), **Standardise** (develop a system to standardise the activities of housekeeping) and **Sustain** (maintain a system by audit and review). 5S is a concept to keep everything simple. This can be applied everywhere including offices, houses, temples, schools and the whole town. The benefits of 5S include a better work environment, less time for searching, a good feeling, reduction of stress with a clutter-free environment, enhanced employee morale, improved safety, and overall enhanced productivity.

Thinking of 5S can be applied in your mind as well like the way it is applied in physical space. The 1st S in this could be to get rid of regrets piling up at one corner, worries littered everywhere, past negative experiences, over expectations from others, old grudges, comparison with others and so on. Emotional cluttering may lead to stress and depression. The challenge today is the overloading of information through social media. Control your time by properly scheduling time to be spent on social media. Mind has unlimited space but because of these unwanted things, you may be left with limited space to operate. How would you keep your mind clean and organized through regular mind detoxification?

Barnacles are pesky creatures that attach themselves to the bottom of boats and propellers, causing the boat to go slow, increase fuel consumption, damage the hull's surface and spoil the boat's appearance. These organisms are removed regularly to make boat navigate better. Similarly, work on removing barnacles attaching to your mind, system and workplace to enhance your productivity.

Some guidelines for being organised to be more productive:

- Keep your working table organised and free from clutter. Keep only the things required and arrange everything neatly. Clean daily. You should be able to retrieve things you need quickly. The environment can influence productivity. In Chinese Feng Shui belief, clutter can affect the flow of energy.
- Develop the habit of keeping your papers and items properly. There should be a logical place for everything.
- Be clear of things pending as of today and corresponding priorities to take up on the next days.
- When you file a paper either as a hard copy or soft copy, have a methodology for fast retrieval later.
- Throw away things you have not used for a long time. It can declutter the area. Eliminate those that do not add value to you. Be selective in buying new things. Buy only those that you really need and use. Many times, less is more.
- Keep things which you use frequently within easy reach.
- Identify the flipside of being overly organised. You may become inflexible which in excess may lead to a sort of behaviour called OCD—**O**bsessive **C**ompulsive **D**isorder.
- Allocate a decluttering and organizing time with regular frequency in your schedule.
- You can use many Apps available in the market to set reminders, fix your schedules, to make a to-do list and monitor your time on social media and so on.
- Whenever you get an idea or insight, note it down immediately in a notebook physically and digitally. You can decide later whether to continue with that lead or drop it.

- Look at your daily routines and reflect on areas to improve to be more organized.
- By being disorganized, you may end up firefighting leading to a waste of time at the cost of quality causing stress. Plan well in advance to avoid this.
- Schedule a slot once a year to reflect on what happened in the previous year and how you did in all spheres of life like skill, knowledge, hobby, finance, family, friends, social connect, professional journey, spirituality, and health. Reflection on this could be a basis for bringing in changes in the subsequent year.

Reap the benefit of being organised in physical and mental space to be more productive. This skill can be acquired through practice. Simplify your life by being more organized.

My top three improvement action points

1.

2.

3.

32
EFFECTIVE USAGE OF YOUR TIME

Time is really the only capital that any human has and the only thing he can't afford to lose
— **Albert Einstein**

Successful persons, unlike ones not successful, can exercise their control over how they use their time, energy, priorities, and schedules. All of us are given only 24 hours per day. On average, 8 hours are spent sleeping and the other 8 hours are spent eating, taking care of hygiene, travelling, leisure activities and so on. You are effectively left with only 8 hours per day to do any productive work. You cannot manage time as there is no way to increase or decrease this commodity. But you can use this invaluable resource that belongs to you more wisely and effectively.

Time is like a flowing river. Flow is unidirectional. Once flown, it is gone. You can touch it only once. This flow cannot be stopped, and it will wait for none. When you were young, you were counting up looking for the next birthday and daydreaming that you would go to college, get into a job, get married and so on. After middle age, you will start counting down as you realise that the end is fixed, though not known, and you are left with only a certain more years on this planet. If you realise this early in life and reflect often that you are given a finite amount of this resource, you will take control of your time yourself not giving remote control to others.

Estimate roughly how many months you may stay on this earth, collect so many numbers of marbles and put them in a glass bowl and keep this in your main hall of the house. Take out one marble from the jar every month and before throwing it, ask yourself how effectively you spent that month. You will start valuing time more.

Imagine that you are given a jar everyday full of precious gems. If not used during the course of the day, it will be written off at the end of the day. How would you use the gems? Of course, you will ensure that not a single gem is wasted without using it. Replace the word gems with time. These gems are 24 hours each day. You are given two jars each day. One with time and another with energy. Use them judiciously. Imagine time as a currency that is allowed to be used only once.

Time and health are two invaluable assets of life that will be valued, unfortunately, only when they are not there. Time is a perishable commodity. Start appreciating its value when it is available to you. No use crying over spilt milk. Time is the most valuable gift from your side to others since you are giving something which you will never get back.

Unproductive use of time is to work faster which leads to more problems or working longer which ends up with no free time and with physical and mental health issues. Within the available time of the day, decide with the right priority what to do and what not to do. Leaving undone non-essential ones is also an art to manage time. Success in using time effectively lies in your choices. Working hard without direction is unproductive.

One of the strong excuses you hear to do a job is the shortage of time. This is far from the truth. The issue will be that it is not the availability of time but the usage of the time without the right priority. There is a relationship between time and commitment.

Parkinson's law says, "Work extends to the extent of time availability." Sometimes, a shortage of time can be more productive, when you will focus on really what is important.

"Make sure where your time goes," said Peter Drucker. If you identify where you are wasting your time in the course of the day, where you are engaging in work which you should not have done at all and other non-value-added activities, you will start valuing time. Start identifying wastage of time including taking feedback on your behaviours leading to wastage of time. You can focus on using time more effectively to do the necessary work, ones that take you in the direction where you want to move.

Some signs of behaviours that indicate that you are not using time effectively are not finding things easily, missing appointments, last-minute rescheduling, being unprepared for meetings, being unable to concentrate, having messy desks and cluttered files, volunteering to do things other people are supposed to do, in firefighting mode most of the time, looks tired and confused and always showing to be busy. Are any of these applicable to you?

By thinking about and planning activities ahead, time can be saved. Without planning, you will end up doing things as they come up, which may end up as not optimum usage of time. Do daily, weekly, and monthly planning and schedule appropriately. Plan your day the night before.

IKEA's founder gave a good hint to realize the value of each minute. He prescribes dividing your time into slots of 10 minutes. Plan and monitor the utilization of each slot.

Follow Pareto's 80-20 principle of vital few and trivial many, which says 80% of accomplishments come from 20% of activities. Focus on those 20% significant activities where you should spend time. Using your time may not bring results, but doing the activities of high priority, which will take you towards your goal, will surely bring results.

A day's activities can be grouped into four categories: improvement, routine or maintenance, ineffective and wasteful. Make time to focus on improvement activities supporting your growth. Delegate or automate a portion of routine activities and be watchful to reduce ineffective and wasteful activities.

You cannot be fully productive by using time well alone. In the time spent on an activity, look at the level of your intensity in the work. Intensity includes right priority, mindset, emotional level, focus without disturbance and so on. Work on using time as well as intensity to be more productive.

Reflect now on what you did in the last hour. Did you engage in activities that were meaningful for you, how effectively you used that time and what changes would you like to make in the next hour to be more productive? If you do this every hour, no one can beat you in using time effectively.

My top three improvement action points

1.
2.
3.

33

ARE YOU FEELING FULFILLED?

To have an extraordinary quality of life, you need two skills: The science of achievement and the art of fulfilment

– Tony Robbins

Feeling that your abilities and talents are being fully used is one definition of being fulfilled. It is a sense of feeling satisfied within you. Each one of you is a different and unique individual and the inner condition of each one is different. There cannot be another person like you. Fulfilment for you is something unique and personal for you. You need to take responsibility and accountability for the choices you make for your fulfilment. Enhancing fulfilment is a personal and subjective inner journey. Fulfilment being a personal journey, what works for one person may not work for the other person. Find your own pathways that make you feel fulfilled.

You will feel fulfilled when you have spent your time well. Be in the present moment with full attention. You are at your best when you live in the present and experience every second. Life happens in the present. Have you noticed that you feel joy and lose a sense of time when you do things you like most? The other way around, you feel that the needle of the clock is not moving when you must do a job that is not your cup of tea and the one you do not like doing. Find something to do that gives you joy, excitement, energy, and enthusiasm. Engage in practices that promote mindfulness.

If you do something you feel is meaningful, you are very passionate about it, and this will touch the lives of others directly or indirectly, when you help others and they progress from that, you feel fulfilled. Volunteer for causes that resonate with you. A good life is not a self-centred life, it is said. One of the company owners told me that he finds joy when he sees the prosperity of the family of his employees more than he does with the money he makes out of his business. He has a sense of satisfaction that he is contributing to society and he does not mind travelling the extra mile for that.

At the end of the day, think about doing which work during the day makes you feel satisfied and makes you sleep deeply and look forward to getting up happily tomorrow morning. The expression of gratitude for all the good things that happened improves your mental stamina, energy, positivity, sleep, and overall happiness. Reflect deeply if you are feeling why the morning comes.

Long-term fulfilment and well-being come from relationships and connecting with the people around you including relatives and friends. Lonely people feel unfulfilled. How much time are you spending to build and nurture relationships? Positive relationships will boost your emotional energy. Be compassionate and show kindness to others.

When you feel fulfilled and happy, you will perceive the events and situations differently and you are likely to commit yourself to making the next moment better.

Fulfilment of life comes from having a vision or dream and aligning towards that intensively. Dhirubhai Ambani, successful businessman of India, a story of rag to rich, built the empire of

Reliance Industries, dreamt and visualized the growth of Reliance as an integral part of the grand vision of India. He was convinced that India could become an economic superpower in the world and Reliance could play an important role in realizing this. He did not give up and continued to work on his dream despite his health issue with a major stroke. He got fulfilment by seeing many millionaires from Reliance Industries and thousands of families getting employed. His goals were aligned with his aspirations.

Never stop learning, as life never stops teaching. You are dead when you stop learning. Keep yourself alive with a constant desire to explore new things, experience, and later express yourself. Be ready to embrace the unknown and get out of your comfort zone. When you start identifying your potential and work on exploiting it to the extent possible, you will feel fulfilled. Take up a challenge that will test your capabilities. Be ready to face hurdles and do everything to overcome them. A lot of people climb Mount Everest, knowing well the challenge involved. They knowingly take the risk of dying in the process. They get joy and excitement from stretching themselves beyond their limits. Continuously work on personal growth and development.

You will get unfulfilled when your actions do not align consistently with your core values. Values are those ideals that matter to you the most. Set goals in alignment with your core values. Live life to keep up the core values you believe in, and you will feel fulfilled.

Often practice self-reflection to understand your values, strengths, and passions. Check to ensure your actions and choices truly align with what you want from life. This brings clarity on the steps to be taken next including corrections.

Embrace challenges and failures as opportunities for growth and learning. Don't be afraid of failures. Rather see them as stepping-stones towards success. The process of overcoming obstacles and challenges from setbacks can contribute to personal fulfilment and resilience.

Holistic happiness, consisting of happiness in the areas of health, emotions, finance, spirituality, relationship, careers, competencies, hobbies and so on, helps to attain self-fulfilment.

Be patient with yourself and keep on exploring to find what truly brings you joy and fulfilment in your career and life. Fulfilment comes by focusing more on your inside world than on the outside world. A life of joy and happiness is worth living than a life of any number of physical possessions.

I conclude with the saying of Bob Dylan, American singer on success, "A person is a success if he gets up in the morning and gets to bed at night and in between does what he wants to do." Choose to do a task happily instead of a 'have to do' mindset to feel more fulfilled.

My top three improvement action points

1.

2.

3.

34

MANAGING YOUR EMAILS

Quality over quantity – Emails may be cost efficient but it's no excuse to not produce quality content to give to a targeted audience

– Benjamin Murray

Despite so many communication tools in the market, email continues to be a preferred communication tool, especially in business circles. We see a lot of people wasting time with emails without managing them properly. Email is meant to enhance our productivity and should not be a hindrance to it. You should learn the art of handling this powerful tool to your advantage. It may be worth relooking and unlearning some of the habits developed over a period in dealing with emails.

You may want to look at the following points that will enhance productivity by dealing with emails more effectively:

- Do not allow your inbox to be cluttered with so many emails. Read regularly to delete junk and unwanted ones.
- Unsubscribe unnecessary emails that adds no value to you. Email is a push communication tool and many advertising agencies and newsletters try to push on their unsolicited message to you.
- Set folders to move high and low-priority emails, ones that are to be preserved for taking action later. These folders may be

assigned names like to be scheduled, to act right away and needed for later reference.
- Set a discipline for yourself on the frequency of seeing emails and where to see them (on laptop, PC or mobile). Seeing emails on mobile as they arrive is a great distraction. Constant engagement with them can be a killer of time. Do not keep the email box open always and turn off its notifications.
- Do not develop the habit of looking at emails first in the morning. It can set a wrong priority for the day. If your business or job demands to see them first, look at only critical ones.
- Do not develop the habit of responding to all emails immediately after receipt. Though it looks good, it can be a distractor of time. If it is going to be a short reply, you may go ahead and do so or otherwise, you can schedule a time for responding if an email demands time to respond. It is a good practice to respond to the other person when you will revert.
- Keep autoresponder on with a message when you are not using email for a period. It helps others not to send unnecessary reminders.
- Keep proper subject lines for each mail you send. It helps in storing and retrieval later. It will also help to draw the attention of the receiver.
- When you write an email, be very specific, crisp, and focused with clarity of what you want to say and what to expect from others. This will reduce email traffic for the same subject. Respect other people's time.
- Do not respond to emails copied to you unless it is really required. If you are not adding value, inform the sender of topics where you are not required to be marked.
- If you are part of the group mail and these messages are not adding value, ask the administrator to delist your email.
- Remember that email is not a replacement for phone calls. Do not use emails to send too many reminders. It may be irritating. Pick up the phone.

- Look at your spam folder regularly and do not open suspicious emails.
- Do not forward emails with jokes and other content which will waste others' time. They will reciprocate this.
- Before pressing the send button, read the contents again for any corrections. Typing it right the first time saves time.
- Conduct housekeeping of the mailbox by deleting all old mails that are not needed.
- You can use the calendar feature to set a reminder to reply to a mail received or to remind for feedback for the sent ones.
- Use proper font and size in emails for better readability. All capital letters in the mail are not good and avoid using different colours unless it has a purpose.
- Emails are not the right media for communicating a message where emotions are involved. Consider face-to-face meetings, video calls or phone calls.
- Check the spelling, grammar, structure, tone and whether formal language is used, before sending. Avoid the usage of emojis.
- Avoid email copies to those who are not really required to be in the loop. You may be wasting their time. Use Bcc appropriately.
- Use the right salutations and usage of the first name or the second name, depending on your relationship with the receiver: Hi, Hello, Dear, Respected, etc.
- If you are sending an attachment, mention that in the email text to draw attention.
- Email is not the right platform to give feedback or criticism, but it is fine for giving appreciation. Words in writing hurt more than they do orally.
- It is a good practice to use an auto signature with your contacts including designation and company instead of ending it with just your name.

By spending 10 minutes per day for better management of email, imagine how much time you will save in a year to do more productive work. There is always scope to improve obvious and known things like email handling to be more productive. See the gap between the way you are handling now and the above points to reflect what changes are needed. If you find a few valuable points, then my writing these tips is worth it.

My top three improvement action points

1.

2.

3.

35

CONTROL YOUR THOUGHTS

Once you replace negative thoughts with positive ones, you'll start having positive results

– Willie Nelson

On an estimate, around 60,000 thoughts come up in our minds every day. Thoughts can be our best friends or worst enemies. By taking control of your thoughts, you can be happier, less stressed, and better equipped to solve problems.

Lucy Mallory, an American writer, said, "Each thought a person dwells upon, whether he expresses or not, either damages or improves his life." Thoughts have life. They are like seeds sown in the field of mind. The seed, positive or negative, grows into a huge tree. An idle mind has more unnecessary thoughts and hence dissipates more energy. This may be the reason that you would be more tiresome on an idle day than on a busy day. It is rightly said that the idle mind is the devil's workshop. Thoughts have an influence on our capability.

Buddhist scripture The Dhammapada mentions the power of thoughts, "What we are today comes from our thoughts of yesterday, and our present thoughts build our life of tomorrow. Our life is the creation of our mind."

In each situation, you get many thoughts, and you have a choice to select them. Imagine that you are scolded by your boss before your subordinates in a meeting. What possible types of thoughts might come up in your mind?

- Positive – I have made a mistake. The boss is right. I should work on it to correct it.
- Negative – The boss is wrong. He should not have done it. What happens to my reputation before others? I am feeling bad. I should defend myself though I know the mistake is mine.
- Useless – The boss does not have better work. I have not done anything wrong. The boss is wrong.
- Toxic – The boss has insulted me. I will take revenge. I will look for an opportunity to give him back.
- Creative – I will take input from my boss later to understand what made him do this. I will work on it and prove to the same team that I am better than others.

In the above situation, your focus and productivity depend on what type of thoughts you entertain and develop further.

Thoughts are your opinion produced from your thinking or occurring suddenly. Buddha said that you are what you think, and you are shaped by your thoughts. Thoughts lead to feelings which in turn give rise to actions that end up as results. So, to improve your results, work on your thoughts. The outside world reflects what happens inside. To succeed, start cleaning inside. This beautiful world is shaped by the thoughts of millions of people. Our personality is shaped by our thoughts.

Negative thoughts will disempower you to take action. Examples of a few negative thoughts could be: the future is not bright, no one can be believed, I am immersed in problems, I am not good enough, I am a weak person, days are tough, business is a mess and so on. With negative thoughts, you feel low and find it difficult to focus on the right actions.

If I instruct you to close your eyes and not think of a white monkey, you will start seeing more white monkeys in your mind. Similarly, negative thoughts cannot be sucked out of the mind. The mind cannot stay in a vacuum. Pump with positive and empowering thoughts to purge negative thoughts. Before going to sleep daily, try to drain all unwanted thoughts, like you drain dirty water from the wash basin. Be aware that you cannot put a fence around your mind to stop negative thoughts from coming in.

The mind is like a computer processor converting inputs to outputs. Output quality depends on input quality. What type of inputs are you giving to your mind daily? You are what you feed into your mind. Reflect on the extent of negative inputs coming to you from newspapers, social media, TV discussions, the internet, and people around you. News which are negative spreads faster and people catch up faster. The media knows this well and they focus on this aspect. Apart from this, the mind by default, continuously gets Automatic Negative Thoughts (ANTS).

A few aspects can help you to control thoughts positively to enhance productivity:

Detach to the extent possible from toxic people, environment, media, unwanted worries, fears, and high expectations. Can you start reducing screen time—mobile, TV, computer—per day? Identify WhatsApp chats including groups that induce negative thoughts and come out.

Develop an attitude of gratitude. Count your blessings and be thankful for all the things you are bestowed already. It is a good practice to write a gratitude journal along with all the positive things that happened during the day.

Incorporate in your routine, reading positive books and listening to inspirational lectures. Have a learning mindset and write down your learnings in the day. This is like giving daily vitamins to the mind to keep it healthy.

Set a goal and work on it. With this, you will be more focused, you will be more conscious on usage of your time and this will shorten your idle time. Idle mind is a devil's workshop to manufacture negative thoughts.

"No one makes you inferior without your consent," said Eleanor Roosevelt, American diplomat and activist. Work on the negative talks that the small voice inside your mind generates. A negative mind cannot have a positive thought. Practice daily positive affirmations to feed your subconscious mind.

Yoga, meditation, mindfulness and breathing practices support the wandering mind to focus and reduce the number of thoughts. Daily investment in this is worth it. They give you physical and mental health.

Watch the words you use daily. This can induce a thought. By looking at a problem, you can develop different types of thoughts by saying, "I am in a mess," "It is an opportunity to learn something," and "I should work on my strength to resolve."

Despite your best efforts, the outcome may turn out to be not intended or even negative. Failures will happen. See how you can take this as a positive experience and move on without losing hope. Being positive in a negative situation does not mean that you keep hoping for situations to be better, but means taking positive actions to set the situation right.

Like everything else in life, we have a choice to nurture positive or negative thoughts. Through practice, you can have control over your thoughts for a better choice and outcome. Quality of life is linked to the texture of your thoughts. Your energy flows where your mind goes.

My top three improvement action points

1.

2.

3.

36

BE LIKE BEES

The busy bee has no time for sorrow

– William Blake

Bees and their behaviour are quoted by many management Gurus in their motivational talks or words. Each bee flies around 600 km in its lifetime to create 1/10th of a spoon of honey. In honeycomb formation, each bee is a contributor. What would this world look like if each one of us, taking lessons from bees, contribute our bit to make the world a better place? If someone is thinking that they are too small to make a difference, they don't know about the contribution of each bee and how a honeycomb is formed.

Bees love to be working without rest and holidays. They don't look at the clock while working. They start their work by six a.m. in the morning and go ceaselessly till sunset. No monitoring of work or taking attendance is required. They know their task very well. That is to extract nectar from flowers and convert it to honey. They keep a small portion of this for themselves, giving the rest to others. It may be difficult to find many who have the mindset of a bee on work with a selfless motto. Bees know how to perform their role effectively.

Teamwork can be learnt from bees, in which they are excellent. Their ability to work as a team keeps the honeycomb strong and safe. Bees follow the principle of "all for one and one for all."

They never work against other bees within the hive. Bees are a good example to say there is strength in unity. Each honeycomb will have a female queen bee and male bees called drones and worker bees. The role of each within the team is well defined. Queen bees lay eggs, drones have the task of mating and worker bees are the ones collecting nectar and protecting the queen. If you are managing a team, to enhance team effectiveness, clearly define the role and responsibility of each team member. The success of the team lies in collective responsibility. Beehive has thousands of bees that may look chaotic. But there is an orderliness in that crowd.

Bees strive to keep their hives extremely clean. They throw out dead larvae, debris, and other wastes from the hive regularly. They work in a clutter-free environment. Taking a lesson from bees, if you keep a clutter-free environment, it contributes to higher productivity.

"Busy as bees" usage is commonly used. They are busy energetically with a single focus and without multitasking. Though honeycombs many have thousands of bees, each is engaged in its own productive work without interfering with others. They share the responsibilities well. All bees will not fly out for collection of nectar. Some stay behind to take care of the home. Each is fully engaged in its work and there is no excuse to escape work or be lazy.

For some reason, bees may be forced to shift their places. It will get adjusted to the new place very fast. If it does not get a place in the forest or on a tree, it will settle on a tall building and start building honeycomb. The changed environment will not have any impact on their daily routines. If the number of bees in the honeycomb increases, it will work on increasing its house size. Otherwise, it will not expand the house for the sake of accumulating more honey. The bees are not greedy.

The bees show the highest respect for their leader, i.e., the queen bee. If the leader decides to shift the place, all bees just follow it without questioning. No bee demonstrates its superiority, and each will carry out its work as a disciplined soldier. This is the secret to why there is no quarrel among bees.

Bees are a good example of selfless service. It does not do a work thinking about what benefit it will derive from it, but works with the attitude of helping others. The bees involuntarily support cross-pollination which is essential for genetic variation, increasing plant diversity and adaptability in changing environments. The result is healthier seeds and new plant varieties. Bees prepare honey from the nectar of flowers, which has tremendous medicinal value. Even though they work so hard, what they consume in the process is only a fraction of the honey they produce and distribute the rest to society. They spend their entire life distributing sweets in the form of honey to others. What a splendid philosophy really!

Bees are brilliant engineers. In a honeycomb structure, the hexagon shape, unlike a square or triangle, will hold more amount of honey with the same consumption of material. Best usage of resources.

"If bees only gathered nectar from perfect flowers, they wouldn't be able to make even a single drop of honey," says Mastshona Dhliwayo, a Canada-based philosopher. This would mean that bees do not discriminate and identify that every flower has something good to offer. What a wonderful way of looking at only the positives!

Bees are a good example to show that being busy should have a purpose. Mosquito is also busy, but no one praises it. If you are busy, reflect on busy for what. Bees are so busy that they do not have time to worry. Apart from being kind to the selfless creature bee, think over what amazing lessons you can learn from bees in the area of focus, dedication, hard work, teamwork and selfless service, to be more productive.

My top three improvement action points

1.

2.

3.

37

PRODUCTIVITY IN ORAL COMMUNICATION

Communication is the solvent of all problems and is the foundation for personal development
— **Peter Shepherd**

When hiring a new person for the company, it is said one should look at the **ACE** of the person in the same order. **A** stands for attitude, **C** for communication and **E** for expertise. Communication takes a higher position than expertise. One may be brilliant, an expert in the domain and intelligent, but if he or she is not able to communicate effectively, success is not possible. Leaders are good communicators. A person starts communicating directly or indirectly, verbally, or non-verbally from the time of birth till the last breath. This one skill, part of general competencies, is needed in every type of job. Mastering the art of communication will contribute to an increase in productivity. You might have observed in companies, organizations, or associations where there is a loss of productivity, though difficult to quantify exactly, due to poor communication, wrong communication, vague communication, untimely communication, over-communication, miscommunication, and no communication.

The first choice for effective communication is to decide which channel should be used. Channels can be letters, WhatsApp or

SMS, E-mails, phone calls, video conferencing or face-to-face meetings. Each channel has advantages or disadvantages. Decide the right channel considering the situation for a positive impact. Wrong channel selection can be unproductive. Sometimes, a combination of channels may be warranted.

Effective communication is a two-way exchange process that involves active listening free of stress, usage of feedback, concise and clear transfer of messages with appropriate body language wherever necessary and with accountability by the speaker or sender and listener or receiver.

Areas that can come in the way of your communication are lack of clarity on what to include and exclude, urge to share more than needed, not considering the receiver's point of view, presumption, no active listening, inadequate preparation, emotional disturbances, not recognising receiver's comprehension level including language issues, usage of too many jargons, order of presentation, 'I know all' feeling and not using the right channel of communication. Reflect on the areas to work on.

Be explicit in communication to avoid any misunderstanding. For example, instead of saying, "I will meet you tomorrow," be explicit by mentioning the purpose, at what time and where to meet, points to discuss and how long. With this, the discussion will be more productive.

Communication is not about using jargon. Express in a simple language clearly, audibly and in a crisp way, so that the other person can comprehend well. Always think ahead about what you are going to say and how you are going to say that. An overload of information is detrimental to communication. Pause in between to check the understanding of the receiver.

As a listener, pay undivided attention to the speaker and look at the face, encourage the speaker to say fully what he or she wants to say and mentally summarise your understanding at the end. Making notes of important points is a good practice.

Dalai Lama has said this beautifully about listening: "When you talk, you are only repeating what you already know. But if you listen, you may learn something new."

Effective communication is 80% preparation and 20% actual communication. Preparation includes purpose, planning and practice. This is applicable to both oral and written communications. Know more about the person receiving your communication.

Tailor's rule works here, "Measure twice and cut once." The cost of correction of poor communication is higher. Follow the "do it right the first time" principle.

Learn to neutralise the feelings from previous interactions. The residue of emotions from previous conversations may have an impact on the effectiveness of current communication. Taking a pause and deep breath between two different conversations will help in managing this. The practice of mindfulness contributes to neutralising emotions.

While you communicate, do not expect the other person will agree with your point. Accept the differences of opinions, feelings and ideas, and work together to come to a common understanding. Encourage the other person to ask questions and voice their thinking.

Usage of I-message gets connected well with others. For example, instead of saying, "You are wasting my time," you can say, "I am under time pressure." It is a way to express your feelings and views without attacking the other person. It demonstrates equality and fairness with others and is very powerful in resolving conflicts.

Communication can act as a wall or as a bridge depending on the type of words you use. Instead of saying, "You should do this," is it not better to say, "Can you consider doing this?" or "Is there a way to do it?" No one likes commands.

Do not speak too fast or too slow. You will be perceived differently. A person who speaks too slow will be viewed as a passive person, hesitant and not confident and the one too fast will be seen as an aggressive, impatient, and egotistic person.

The tone has more impact than the words. How you say matters more than what you say. Do not speak rudely and be polite. Someone has beautifully said that those who speak rudely cannot sell honey and those who speak sweetly can sell chillies.

In business communications, be specific and with facts, unlike in social communications which are generic in nature and mainly based on opinions.

On the timing and frequency of communication, James Clear recommends, "It's generally better to over-communicate. If you wait to reply because you don't have an answer yet or because you don't want to share bad news, the other party often ends up making assumptions about what the delayed reply might mean. Silence frustrates and confuses people. Better to communicate early and often."

Work on your communication skills, without which, your advancement in your career is limited despite your best technical capabilities.

My top three improvement action points

1.

2.

3.

38

DO YOU WORK LIKE A HARE OR TORTOISE?

It does not matter how slowly you go as long as you do not stop

- Confucius

All of you have heard Aesop's fable on the race between hare and tortoise. In this race, the hare ran very fast in the beginning and took a rest in the last stretch. The tortoise was slow but steady. With this, the tortoise won the race. The tortoise never stopped during the race. The moral of the story is that slow and steady wins the race. The same thing applies to productivity. Slow and steady should be clubbed to find a meaning to this.

Dave Ramsey, an American radio personality, articulated, "We live in a culture full of hares, but the tortoise always wins."

When I was a professor of practice at a university, I observed the behaviour of hares and tortoises with students while they do a six-month project as a part of master's degree fulfilment. At the beginning of the project, nothing would happen in the first two months, as the thinking was that 'there is enough time left for the completion'. Later, the project slowly starts and gets accelerated one month before the deadline. In that period, there would be hectic activities till the binding of project reports and final presentations. I used to get pressured at the last minute for review sessions before finalizing. The results of such type of work ended up with the inadequate quality of conclusion, hurriedness to complete, stress, and lack of preparation for the final interview and presentation.

Students who followed a linear approach with time by putting in the right corresponding steady efforts did better. I also saw a few students who were very enthusiastic and energetic at the beginning of the project and slowly lost tempo over the period. Consistent efforts were not seen with many of them. When some progress was made, they would tend to rest or slow down and, as a result, they would end up doing a lot of things at the last minute. I believe that a better approach would be to put in higher efforts at the beginning of the project when there would be enough time and less pressure, depending on other schedules, and later keep the required tempo for completion. This would help with any last-minute changes and uncertainties.

In the current dynamic market, you may think that you are pushed to run like a hare. You hear sayings like 'Darwin's theory of survival of the fittest' should be changed now to 'survival of the fastest.' No question about the need for speed. The right question is how long can you run like a hare without getting exhausted? I am not endorsing becoming slow or less agile in response to change. Instead of running like a hare at the last minute as a response to the change, why not adopt the mindset of a tortoise with slow and steady adaption to the change? This is possible if one starts the change activities soon after the sensing needs to change.

Efforts can be slow but should be steady. If you want to get the benefit of meditation, sitting for a few hours on the first day, skipping the second day, and half an hour the third day will not give enough results. Instead, even ten minutes of meditation daily without skipping will give better results. The same thing is applicable to reading, exercising, tasks of a project etc.

Jim Rohn, American entrepreneur used to say, "Success is nothing more than a few disciplines, practiced every day." He is talking of the tortoise mindset for success.

As an example, if you want to improve your health, start with small physical exercises daily with consistency. With practice over a period, your identity will shift as a person who cares for health. With this identity, you will not give up daily exercise. Then increase the intensity. Consistency first before intensity.

To enhance productivity in manufacturing, the Japanese use three words called **3M**s, namely **M**uda, **M**ura, and **M**uri. Muda are wastes, meaning activities and resources which will not add value to customers but only add cost to the system. Muri is an overburden on the system. One may think that by making employees work ten hours daily, Muda can be reduced. But what about the stress created and likely lack of quality and slowdown that will affect productivity? Another question is how long they can work like this. So, reducing Muda with Muri is not a good solution. The third element is Mura with the meaning of "Unevenness, irregularity, non-uniform and inequality." It is about the absence of the rhythm. One example in the context- Mura is present when one person works for 10 hours per day, 3 hours the next day, off on the other day and so on. Owing to this, productivity will come down. Variation is considered an enemy of quality. Japanese prescribe that Muri be addressed first, then Mura and finally Muda. Ideal will be no Mura, no Muri, and no Muda. How can you apply these 3Ms in your work?

Nature is slow and steady in its growth. It works like a tortoise. When you are consistent, you are disciplined to be on the way towards the goal. Do a bit every day to move in the direction of your goal. Slow progress is better than no progress. Slow work should not be seen as unproductive if you are focused, involved, thoughtful, and consistent. Be afraid and concerned about standing still on the way. Stay on track without giving up. Progress has more to do with direction than with speed. Hurrying is a sickness.

My top three improvement action points

1.

2.

3.

39

LIMIT YOUR OVERTHINKING

Overthinking is just a painful reminder that you care way too much even when you shouldn't

— **Anonymous**

Thinking is good but overthinking is not considered positive and is an unhealthy habit. Anything in excess is poison. The same applies to overthinking. Overthinking is one of the factors for unhappiness. It is the art of creating problems that do not exist. You would have seen many people who have mastered the art of overthinking and can mess up with the situation as well as with the result. With overthinking, you will worry and dwell upon something repeatedly and keep it in mind for a long time. Such people find it difficult to forget and move on and in extreme cases, will end up with anxiety, depression, and other mental health disorders. Overthinking can contribute to loss of sleep, poor concentration, lack of interest, and loss of memory and may lead to a tendency to go to shells, keep away from people, blame themselves, punish themselves and be under pressure always. Instead of solving problems, they end up running around issues without any logical conclusion. Overthinking is a demotivator and may prevent you from doing anything.

When an incident happens, it is normal to analyse the positive and negative aspects of the incident. Matured persons live in the present and move on without dwelling too much on what happened. I came across an employee who behaved badly with his boss. It was an act of knee-jerk reaction to a situation. Naturally, he felt bad later. That is normal. But this person was repenting for this incident much longer and did not try to forget. He would bring up this point again and again. A sort of guilt syndrome occupied his mind with overthinking about the same incident. It would have been better if he had apologised to his boss for his bad behaviour and had worked on keeping his emotions in control. But he rather started feeling bad about himself and tried to avoid other seniors. He found it difficult to forget the incident. Overthinking made this person lose some portion of mental energy contributing to the loss of productivity.

Mistakes are bound to happen and sometimes strong negative emotions will hit us. Instead of dwelling on the emotions for a long time, we should learn to feel the emotion fully and come back to normalcy as quickly as possible. Overthinking about fear of failure and something unforeseen that may come up on the way may stop you from taking action.

What could be the reasons for overthinking? It could be from unknown fear, tendency to be perfect, social or family pressure to perform, childhood negative experiences, lack of confidence and self-consciousness.

You can overcome overthinking by being aware and with practice. Allocate 15-20 minutes per day as worry time instead of worrying the whole day. In this slot, watch your mind and reflect on what you are overthinking about and why, and what actions you can take. It is a good practice to write down all your worries, thoughts and what you can do about it. This exercise will make you light.

Change your perspective on the situation and things will start changing. If your efforts have not given the intended results, instead of being anxious, think about what went wrong and what are the lessons from it. With this perspective, you will see each of your efforts as an experiment to get results or lessons. You are a winner in either case. During the Covid pandemic, when many were worried about the end of life, a few saw opportunities in the situation and looked for ways to adapt to the change.

Learn to excuse and be more compassionate to yourself and to others. Don't suffer for mistakes made by you and give concession to yourself. If your mistakes have hurt someone, seek an apology and move further. You can come out of guilt feeling when you understand that each incident is a contributor to your experience and part of the learning process. Learn to see the positive things that happened from the incident.

If you are overthinking, share with a few with whom you are confident about what is going on in your mind and seek their input. You can look for a coach or mentor to get a different perspective. There is nothing wrong with seeking advice from psychologists or psychiatrists and getting treatment if needed.

If you are a person having "what if" syndrome like "What if I fail?" or "What if my business does not grow?" reframe this to, "What if I win?" "What if my business grows well?" This gives you positive emotions, motivating you to move. Also find your answer to your initial questions with, "Then, I will do…"

Being in the present without allowing your mind to drift to the past or future is one way to reduce overthinking. Practices like deep breathing, mindfulness, yoga, meditation, and being with nature will help. Realise that the past is dead, and the future is unborn. Thinking about them too much will only spoil the present.

Identify things you enjoy doing and can develop them into a hobby. Schedule sometime in the week for them. They are called "mini springs" in your routine, and they rejuvenate your energy. Start learning new things. By this, you are away from thoughts that might trigger overthinking and stress also will come down.

Think of your past successes and wins and how you have overcome your struggles to reach success. This will increase your confidence and support you to stop overthinking about negative consequences.

Everything, including nectar, can be poisonous if in excess. Limit your overthinking and move forward. Thoughts can lead to anxiety. Don't try to control everything and learn to let go. Keep your mind free from things that don't really help you.

My top three improvement action points

1.

2.

3.

40

MAKE A WONDERFUL DAY

Every single day is a good day, no matter how bright or dark it is, because it always brings an opportunity to start a positive beginning in your life.

– **Edmond Mbiaka**

My friend, Madhu, sent me a WhatsApp message recently and, in the end, he wrote, "Make a wonderful day." What a great way to convey greetings, and it made me think a little deeper.

When you say, 'Good Morning,' 'Good Evening,' or 'Good day,' are you expecting morning, evening, or day to be good always? What happens when your day is not that good for various reasons? Would you still say Good Morning or Good Evening? Are you hoping for the day to be good? Will you make some efforts to make the day good? Though these salutations are meant to wish others, view the impact it makes on yourself.

There are three types of people. The first category is pessimists. For them, nothing works, and no good things will happen. They greet others with a 'good morning' mechanically, but in their mind, they are thinking of their fate with negativity. The pessimistic ones talk about problems but don't do anything to solve them. They may be cynical about the surroundings and system. The second category of persons is optimistic ones. They hope good things will happen and believe that by saying 'good morning,' that day would be good for themselves and others. Sounds good, but the issue is that they only hope without doing anything to make things good. Optimism without corresponding actions will not give any results. The third category of people is called realistic ones. These persons not only understand the reality or situation of the day but make efforts to make the day good. They believe that it is in their hands to make a wonderful day. If this does not happen for some reason, they don't mind and take those happenings positively, which are not in their control.

As someone rightly said, maturity is when you work on things in your control and are gracious to accept things not in your control. You may try, if feasible, by influencing things not in control to bring in your control to the extent possible. Instead of waiting for something to happen, work on making it happen. The choice lies with you to decide which type of person you want to be. Your interpersonal relationship with others is affected positively or negatively depending on your choice.

TODAY can be expanded as **T**his is an **O**pportunity to **D**o **A** work better than **Y**esterday. This is a Kaizen mindset. If you do not make use of this wonderful today, soon it will become yesterday. Today is auspicious to make a beginning of things you could not do earlier. There is a Chinese saying which means that there are two occasions to grow trees. One was twenty years ago and the second one is today. Today is an opportunity to sow seeds for tomorrow.

Robert Louis Stevenson, British Author and Adventure novelist, has wonderfully said, "Don't judge each day by the harvest you reap, but by the seeds you plant."

Alexander the Great was discussing with ministers and the military to expand his kingdom. When all were discussing the plan or approach, the king said that if we delayed even by one day, we might lose so much land and commanded us to start with the mission right today. A sense of urgency to make a beginning even in a small way gives a good dividend. I am not undervaluing the power of planning but trying to give a message that today is a wonderful day to make a beginning.

Each one of you is given a choice to make or mar the day as you get up each day. What would be your thinking and attitude in making the day? How the day turns out is based on these. Look at a few choices of expressions in the day:

- Today, I can complain because the weather is bad with rain, or I can be thankful that our plants are getting watered.
- Today, I can grumble about my bad health or rejoice that I am surviving.
- Today, I can complain that I have to go to work, or I can feel grateful that I have a job to take care of myself and my family.
- Today, I can cry that roses have thorns, or I can celebrate the beauty of nature, that thorns have roses in between.
- Today, I can feel bad that I do not have anything to do, or it is an opportunity for me to sit quietly and reflect deeply.

Along with the lips that pray and hope for good things, ensure movement of hands and legs through actions. Be like a sculptor to shape the day you want. Everyone in this world is given the same 24 hours a day. Successful persons have mastered the art of using today wonderfully with the right attitude and priority without postponing tomorrow. If you don't take control of how today should go, it may end up in some way which may not be in the way that you wanted it to be. God helps those who help themselves. As said, yesterday is an expired cheque, tomorrow is a promissory note, and today is a hard currency. Encash this fully.

The alphabet O is absent in YESTERDAY but available in TODAY and three times in TOMORROW. O stands for opportunity which is available today to exploit with the hope of more of it tomorrow.

Madhu's message reminded me to be realistic and take proactive actions to work on those things which are in my control to make the day a wonderful one. Every day is a good day. How can you make today the most beautiful day of your life? As today unfolds, it gives a lot of possibilities to choose from. You are what you choose. Today may not be best for you but you can take action to avoid making it worse. Shaping yourself the way you want starts today. How much goodness can you take out from today? Will you start using and thinking proactively, 'Make a wonderful day' instead of 'Have a wonderful day?'

Thank you, Madhu. Make a wonderful day.

My top three improvement action points

1.

2.

3.

41

MANAGE CONFLICTS CONSTRUCTIVELY

> *An association of men who will not quarrel with one another is a thing which never yet existed*
> **– Thomas Jefferson**

When you interact with people, disagreement on an idea or a project is bound to happen at some point in time. In some cases, conflicts may end up with battles, fights, strained relationships, and prolonged struggle. Contradiction is part of the game. You cannot find someone who can think exactly like you. The length of each of our fingers is different. So also, about people. The perspective of each person is different because of different upbringings, different levels of ego, social influence, belief in different values, different personalities, leadership styles, past experiences, and the level of intelligence. Within yourself, you will get conflicting ideas. Coping with the conflicts within you and with others is a must for progress.

Some extent of conflicts especially in a team, can bring in a lot of benefits. What will the output of the team be if all the team members are thinking alike? Conflicts in a team will enhance creativity and innovation, clarification of core issues, individual and team identity, increase cohesion among team members, understanding of others' points of view, personal growth and change, and challenge thinking and beliefs. On the flip side, if conflicts are not addressed properly, it can lead to stress in team members, unresolved anger, demotivation, loss of energy and enthusiasm, erosion of self-esteem, inefficiency, and productivity loss.

In the situation of conflicts, many responses will come out. It could be a fight by justifying the stand, flight by running away or avoiding, simply following as a victim, compromising to avoid any complications, shutting down by getting into a shell or collaborating to find a win-win situation. Each option has its own consequences. See what works well, depending on the situation.

You are likely to have more conflicts with people who are complainers, know-it-all experts, indecisive, unresponsive ones, micromanagers, impolite ones, busy managers who don't have time for you, negative persons, and perfectionists. You cannot change what they are but can find ways to deal with them in conflicts.

In a company that I was supporting, a conflict came up between the head of marketing and the head of new product development on what should be the priority for developing products. Both of them had their own goals. Emotional outbursts in the meeting, blaming games, and sarcastic emails started flowing. The marketing head's viewpoint was that he had pressure from customers to develop a set of products first, overriding others and the new product development head felt that they had a sequence of development and that cannot be changed at random. The result of this conflict was unhappy subordinates, loss of engagement, loss of time and ultimately unhappy customers. Over a period, this led to an ego clash between the heads of two departments. The operation head had to intervene to resolve this conflict. He called each of them together and listed down all the concerns each had in detail and the impact of those on the business, company, customer, and team. This meeting brought a lot of clarity to them, and they started understanding others' views. Both agreed to enhance their mutual communication through regular meetings to resolve issues jointly. Simple communication can do wonders to resolve conflicts. That is why it is rightly said, "Communication can create a wall or a bridge between people."

Manage your emotions in times of conflict. Negative emotions will make the situation worse, blocking all possibilities to resolve. Take control of emotions, look into the realities and focus on solutions instead of dwelling upon problems and issues. Negative emotions are not bad but staying in that state for long can be harmful. Deep breathing and taking a break may help to regain composure.

Resolve conflict as early as possible before it starts worsening. At the time of conflicts, involve all the people concerned. Find the right place and time where there will be no distractions. Establish the ground rules before starting a discussion. Allow people to vent their feelings and give equal opportunities for all to express themselves without getting angry or showing disrespect to others. Describe the conflicts and how they can have an impact on the business and all stakeholders. Keep the discussion focused on the real core issue and do not allow persons to shift to other topics. Take the ideas from all, brainstorm and agree on steps that meet the requirements of all concerned. Confront situations and not people. Later, ensure that those steps are implemented and followed. Wait to see if the conflicts are resolved. You may have a review meeting later for a complete resolution, including bringing new steps. Continuously take feedback from those concerned.

Aspects that will resolve conflicts are avoiding blame games, focusing on issues and not on persons, emotional management, active listening, appreciation of diversity, no criticism, no judgement, focus on present & future and not on the past, empathy, direct communication, diplomacy, care in using the right words, focusing on the core issue, responding and not reacting, assertiveness, belief that everyone has a good intention and nobody is deliberately creating issues and looking for win-win outcomes.

Ask appropriate questions to make sure you have understood the situation well. Avoid accusatory 'why' questions. Restate to make clear that you have understood what the other person means and wants. Acknowledge a person's feelings and perceptions. Do not ask them to feel differently and work on behavioural change only.

Emotional blockage may lead you to avoid conflicts and procrastinate decision-making. This will hinder you as a leader in dealing with tough decisions. Work on emotional fortitude, which helps you face disappointment, adversity and difficulty courageously.

Persons with fixed mindsets talk about the traits or personality of the other person as the reasons for the conflicts between them instead of confronting the situation. Understand that each person has his own flaws, imperfections, beliefs, and perspectives. Accept these aspects and move on to find a common agreement to address the situation.

Conflicts are part and parcel of your personal and professional life. Understanding them and managing them constructively can contribute to your and your team's productivity.

My top three improvement action points

1.

2.

3.

42

WORK ON UNPRODUCTIVE FORCES

When driving life's road, keep your foot on the gas, don't drive in the reverse, and don't let speed bumps slow you down

– Sonya Parker

You must have heard or read stories which say that there are two types of jackals in our minds. One is black colour, and the other is white. They always quarrel among themselves. Which one will win? Naturally, the one that you feed more. The black jackal represents a negative mindset, and the white jackal represents a positive mindset.

Similarly, two sets of forces are working within you related to productivity. One is a positive one. These forces enhance your productivity. Examples could be working on your priorities, planning, improving your energy level, improving internal motivation, enhancing your focus, working on relationships and so on. These are like white jackals that must be fed more and nurtured continuously and consciously. Positive, productive forces will get you faster in your journey towards success. It is like pressing the accelerator pedal while driving the car. All these positive forces are important to nurture for progress, and time must be allocated to work on these. These are the ones you tend to put off doing less productive activities which are less important.

What about the counterproductive or unproductive forces that will pull you back from being productive? You may be nurturing them unconsciously without being aware of their impact on your success. Examples could be spending more time on TV debates, spending hours each day on social media platforms, gossiping, multitasking, etc. While you want to drive your car faster, observe the speed bumps laid on the lane, which are countering the speed at which you can drive. Work on removing such road speed bumps to enable the car to go faster.

I remember my discussion with the managing director of a multinational company where I worked for many years. We used to meet formally once a month to discuss departmental progress, work-related issues, people development and so on. When we were discussing the role of a leader, he said that a leader must allow his or her people to run, and his or her job is to remove obstacles or bottlenecks on the way. People are capable, and they will run if the leader makes an effort to clear the way. When you lead yourself, identify the obstacles on the way. What you are doing here is, essentially, removing unproductive forces coming in their way to be more productive. Make a list of such positive and negative forces and start working on strengthening and weakening them appropriately.

Michael Porter, a management expert, in his five-force model, explains five forces that are not conducive to growth of the companies and must be taken care of for long-term sustenance. These forces are from customers, suppliers, competitors, new entrants, and substitute products. Companies must work to weaken these forces through counteractions. Otherwise, survival itself may be a challenge in the long term. For clarity, I will touch on the force of substitute products. What happens to the company if your product itself is replaced by another product or becomes superfluous in view of technological advancement? Smart mobile phone has killed many products like camera, alarm clock, compass and so on.

The message here is that companies need to sense the changes happening in the market and work on changing product lines if they see a threat to their existing products itself. Without working on weakening the force of substitute products, the company's growth and even survival may become a challenge. Companies, for their long-term sustenance, must constantly look to address negative forces which may pose risks and look to exploit positive forces, which are opportunities for the growth of the company. Negative forces are risks, and positive ones are opportunities.

Like the above five-force model, what five forces may have negative impacts on your personal productivity that you need to take care of? These forces could be social media, people around, the environment, internal thoughts and force of habit. Reflect on the following questions to be aware of these and later find ways to reduce the impact of the unproductive forces.

- How would you reduce your duration of time on social media, which will cost not only your invaluable time but also disturb your attention and focus?
- How will you be away from people who suck away your energy through their negative talks and opinions?
- How do you avoid circumstances which are not conducive to your personal productivity and create disruptions?
- How will you keep your mind calm not getting disturbed by unnecessary negative imaginations, negative self-talk, fears prompting you not to act and other self-generated negative thoughts?
- How will you act on bad habits acquired over a period and which are killing your productivity?

If you do not work on those unproductive forces to make them weak, they will start working on you. Start sensing empowering (white jackals) and disempowering (black jackals) forces and respond appropriately to enhance personal productivity.

My top three improvement action points

1.

2.

3.

43

CHANGE YOUR PERSPECTIVE

Most misunderstandings in the world could be avoided if people would simply take the time to ask, "What else could this mean?

— Shannon L. Alder

Perspective is the way of looking, understanding and thinking about a situation, experience, issue, or event. It is said that things will change if you change the way you look at things. In the coaching approach, the focus of the coach is to work on changing the perspective of the coachee, so that coachee will start looking at his or her behaviour and the situation differently. If you come across a challenge, how you face it depends on your perspective, "I would better avoid this and run from here" or "I will better see it as an opportunity to test my capability by facing it and learn from it." Your growth depends on the perspective you take on events and situations that happen beyond your control. You will be more accountable and deliver better results in the company you work for if you change your perspective from an employee mindset to an entrepreneur mindset.

Marcel Proust, a French novelist, said beautifully, "Real act of discovery is not in finding new lands but is in seeing with new eyes."

Your perspective changes with time, knowledge, and experience. If you read a book that you read many years ago, it looks different now. There is no change in the book content, but your perspective has changed over the years. With age, my perspective on health, relationships, happiness, money and so on has evolved positively.

The same scene or situation is interpreted differently by different people. I have experienced this many times in my training, where I will show a picture and ask each participant to tell the meaning they got from the picture. I have been amazed at so many diverse views, which are totally different from my perspective.

A scholar was crossing a river in a boat in the evening time when the Sun was about to set. The river was flowing inside the forest. While crossing, he suddenly saw a big fish jumping over the water's surface. With the background of the setting Sun and the splash of water, it was a wonderful scene, and he got inspired to write a poem on this. The scholar asked the boatman to describe the beautiful scene both witnessed. He was expecting appreciation of the scene with beautiful words from the boatman. The boatman said, "Sir, the fish is not less than 10 Kg." See, here is a different perspective of the same scene.

The poet and teacher June Jordan has said on perspective, "Our earth is round, and among other things, that means that you and I can hold completely different points of view and both can be right. The difference in our positions will show stars in your window I cannot even imagine. Your sky may burn with light, while mine, at the same moment, spreads beauty to darkness. Still, we must choose how we separately corner the circling universe of our experience. Once chosen, our cornering will determine the message of any star and darkness we encounter."

My wife and I had to go out of town early in the morning to attend a marriage function. The sun had not yet risen, but there was enough light around to drive without keeping headlights on. As we entered the main road, we saw that the cars coming from opposite sides in another lane had their headlights on. We were talking about why they have kept the lights on when the surrounding sunlight does not demand. My wife started giving a reason, "The drivers of the cars coming from the opposite sides must have started their journey when it was still dark and must be thinking that outside is still dark, or they might have forgotten to put off the headlight. Since we started when the surrounding light was bright enough, there was no need for us to put the headlight on." I agreed with my wife's logic but started thinking, "Is there a possibility that drivers from the other side who are seeing our car may be thinking that we are driving in the dark without headlights on?" You also would have felt the same when you are driving with the headlights on, and opposite vehicles are without the headlights on.

Similar things happen in our life also. In a meeting or in a team, each may be thinking that he is right and why other people are different or may even conclude that other people are wrong. When you meet a new person, you may be in the habit of looking at the other person's light and think why the other person's light is on while yours is off and vice versa. Start appreciating that each can have a different perspective, and without judging, keep driving with or without headlights on, as long as you are driving in the right lane safely without any accident.

To change your perspective, start thinking differently. Change of thinking changes your feelings and corresponding actions. You feel better when you say, "I choose to do this," instead of, "I have to do this." 'Choose' is a choice to embrace empowering you, and "have to" is something forced on you, disempowering you. Reframing is a powerful technique. Change your inner dialogue with yourself. Surround yourself with people and an environment where you stay positive. Psychologists say that any disease can be cured if you change your perspective and start believing that the body is capable of healing itself. The brain, as the head of the symphony, will command each cell of the body and they all will work in a symphony to heal.

I had joint pain in both legs, which lasted many months. Initially, I used to talk about my pain and suffering to everyone I came across and a major part of my energy was lost in focusing on that. This pain started coming down when I changed my perspective, thinking that all other parts of my body were working well and why I should not rejoice about them.

Empathise with others when they behave differently than the way you are expecting. The way you see the world is different from the way they see it. In a recent online meeting, one person joined after thirty minutes of the start. I was upset with him though I didn't talk anything about this. Later, when I talked to him, he said that being late by thirty minutes is very common to him and was not seen as an issue by him. I had to convince him of the impact of his behaviour to change his perspective.

When you focus on the bigger picture, you will start ignoring minor mistakes and failures on your path. Develop your spirit to look at the macro perspective. We see things not as they are but as we are.

Working on the health of mind, emotions, and body will support you to develop a positive outlook towards the world. Your perspective depends on which end of the telescope you are looking from. To make the world look green, start wearing a pair of spectacles with green glass.

My top three improvement action points

1.

2.

3.

44
FOUR I'S OF THE LEADER

Leadership is in action and not a position
– Donald McCannon

For Vidhana Sabha election in Karnataka State in 2023, Prime Minister of India Narendra Modi, came to Bengaluru as a part of the election campaign on behalf of his party. As a part of this, there was a road show where he was taken in an open-top vehicle for 30+ kilometres along a fixed route. As per one estimate, more than one million people witnessed the roadshow. The participants included children, senior citizens, super senior citizens, women, youths, and many disabled persons who came in wheelchairs. All along the road, flowers were showered on Modi by the enthusiastic crowd shouting, "Modi, Modi."

It is very common to conduct roadshows during elections by political parties seeking votes from voters. Many times, for some leaders, we see empty roads during the show and empty chairs in public meetings. For a few rallies and meetings, people are hired from faraway places in buses to give the impression that the leader is important and able to attract a crowd.

Leaving politics and political compulsions for the roadshow, the question that came to my mind was how Narendra Modi was able to draw such a crowd, which is unprecedented. How is he different from other political Leaders?

Did people come to witness the roadshow because he is the prime minister of the country? What was the compulsion and motivation for them to attend? Why many earlier prime ministers and other political leaders were not able to pull such a huge crowd?

Here comes the charisma of a leader to draw people and followers towards him or her. Civil rights activist and Nobel Laureate Martin Luther King Jr., on August 28, 1963, on the steps of the Lincoln Memorial, Washington, DC, USA, gave a speech which is popularly known as the 'I Have a Dream' speech. Tens of thousands of people participated. People came on their own at a time when communication was poor and there was no good facility for transportation. His speech was a call for equality. It identified the faults of America and the measures needed to make it a better place. He talked of many dreams and one of them is that his four children will one day live in a nation where they will not be judged by the colour of their skin but by the content of their character. People came in masses as they believed what Martin believed. They came for themselves and not for him.

A leader is different from a politician. A politician is looking for his personal gains and his or her focus is only till the next elections. Their vision is short-term with an eye of power, and they may end up making false promises to fulfil this. Unlike a politician, a leader looks at the long-term development of the society, the next generation, and the future of the country. A litmus test to find if one is a leader is by asking a question to politicians on their plan for the next generation other than for their sons or daughters. The answer gives clarity.

What would have made the people of Bengaluru to be a part of Modi's Road show on their own, that too on weekends? What leadership qualities of Modi would have attracted them? Why do people not show the same response to other Leaders who also would have done some good work?

I reflected a little deeper on the leadership of Modi. Four I's of leadership play an important role in connecting with people. A good leader should be able to Inspire, Influence, Impact people and take the Initiative to make a difference.

Inspire – By inspiration, people get energised, become enthusiastic and self-motivated. You can inspire people with your energy, self-confidence, standing up to values, readiness to take unexpected challenges, coping with stress, taking responsibility, clarity of vision and goals, futuristic thinking, clarity of communication and following up of words with actions, enthusiasm, ability to connect with people emphatically, oratory skill and maintaining a positive outlook. They were able to see the inspirational qualities of Narendra Modi over a period in social media, TV and newspapers and now have come to see that person physically.

Influence – John C. Maxwell, an American writer, says, "Leadership is influence, nothing more or nothing less." By having influencing quality, you can make others take a decision and act upon it. Your integrity, trustworthiness, emotional bonding with people, credibility, commitment to people, fiscal honesty, making people feel important, showing genuine concern for others, active listening, respecting other's views, positive attitude, proven competence, the way you dress, your personal branding, your body language, being yourself without a mask and what positive aspects others say about you, and so on will support you to develop the ability to influence. A person who can influence by writing, through YouTube, podcasts and so on is also a leader. Modi, in his political career of close to 23+ years, has been able to demonstrate these qualities, and perhaps the crowd was able to connect.

Impact- Leadership is about bringing results. Intention without corresponding actions will not give results and people will be able to identify this gap quickly. The results brought by the leader should have a positive impact on the people. If your actions inspire others to dream more, learn more, do more and achieve more, then you are a leader. Was the crowd able to see the impact of Modi's actions like direct subsidy transfer, GST, infrastructure development, meticulous execution of projects with speed, putting an end to terrorist attacks, digitization and so on?

Initiative- Are you a self-starter? What actions are you taking without someone telling you? How will your initiative inspire, influence and impact others? Are you ready to take risks and come out of your comfort zone? Narendra Modi could have enjoyed all the privileges of the prime minister's position without putting himself at stake in initiatives like the abolition of Article 370, the new vaccine in Corona time, demonetization, etc. Did these qualities inspire and influence people to turn out for his road show?

Leaders make mistakes. They are also human beings. Not all their decisions will give results as expected. They also have biases and limitations. Modi is no exception.

My views above are not to endorse Modi but to reflect on what possibly would have made millions of people witness the road show of Narendra Modi and feel this was their lifetime opportunity.

Leave the debate "whether the roadshow turned out into votes." There are hundreds of factors to win or lose an election. Look at what aspects of Modi as a leader can be benchmarked to develop yourself as a great leader. Which of the I's, do you want to focus on to be a productive leader?

My top three improvement action points

1.

2.

3.

45

MOBILE AND SOCIAL MEDIA AS ENABLERS

It is okay to own technology, what is not okay is to be owned by technology

— **Abhijit Naskar**

One of the current challenges for organizations and individuals is to adopt and adapt to a fast-changing market and world. In Macroeconomics, the word **PESTEL** is used to study changes happening around. **P** for political, **E** for economical, **S** for social, **T** for technological, **E** for environmental, and **L** for legal. These parameters influence us and industries directly or indirectly and there is a need for us to change by understanding the impact and taking actions to adapt. We need to develop a mindset of unlearning and relearning.

The much-debated impacts of technology on us and our children in our day-to-day lives are the internet, smartphones and social media. Everything has two sides. The impacts here are positive as well as negative. There is a set of arguments by Laggards that technology has spoiled us, including human relationships. This is to be seen with a pinch of salt. Technology is an enabler. By itself, it is neither beneficial nor harmful. It all depends on how we use the technology. It is like a knife, which can be used to cut vegetables or to harm ourselves. By using technology judiciously, productivity can be enhanced. No argument that the contribution of technology is very high for the development of the world and has helped to resolve many issues.

Only a few people question if technical development has made us more peaceful and happier. They say that technology can bring more comfort but not happiness. Leaving these arguments apart, let us focus on how we can use smartphones, internet, and social media, which originated from technology as enablers in day-to-day life, to be more productive.

Our so-called constant companion Smartphone has replaced many devices like torches, alarm clocks, compasses, radios, recorders, telephone directories, game gadgets and many others. This device can act as an enabler to increase productivity, provided we understand fully the capabilities of the smartphone and how to use it smartly. A smartphone can make or mar time.

Smartphones, the internet and social media have helped us to be smarter in many ways, and a few of them are:

- Apps are available freely to list out things to do, set the priority and schedule tasks. No more excuse for memory.
- Using social media like LinkedIn, Twitter, Facebook, YouTube, WhatsApp, Telegram, Instagram, and many more helps to connect with others and exchange information on a real-time basis.
- Ideas can be shared through blogs and other social media to connect with people.
- Access to bank accounts from anywhere and usage of wallets for payments digitally.
- Maps with the usage of GPS to navigate to a place.
- Usage of the internet and apps for meditation, games for relaxation, various learnings, planning, collaborating, online purchase, and so on.
- Conduction of conference video calls, webinars, and podcasts

- The Internet is a source of a vast pool of knowledge and information
- Chat GPT is a learning platform which can support making reports

Technology, if not used properly, can hinder progress as well. A few hints in this direction that can hamper your productivity and ways to improve may be worth looking at:

- Do not get too much obsessed with the mobile device. Being overly obsessed may lead to FOMO (Fear Of Missing Out) syndrome, a sort of mental disease. It should not spoil relationships with people.
- Social media can affect relationships. It can be the biggest distraction if not used in a controlled way. Set boundaries of time per day and location. Schedule time for using social media and stop the habit of looking at it all the time.
- A devotee prayed to God intensely, and God appeared and offered to give a boon. The devotee asked for something that can spoil thousands of minds instantaneously. God said, "Granted. Use WhatsApp." On this lighter note, care to use WhatsApp judiciously on spreading or receiving anti-social viruses.
- Negative news spreads faster. Social media is good at making this happen. It can affect a person's ability to judge and make the right decision. Do your homework and use your discretion before believing all the negativity on social media and have a proper perspective.
- Stop all notifications from various Apps. With this, you can focus on the task without disturbances.
- Keep your smartphone away while sleeping. It's better without easy access. This is to avoid the temptation to look at the mobile in between sleep and early in the morning when you get up.
- When you meet a person physically, or travelling with someone or in a meeting, avoid using your smartphone to respect the time

of others and to enable yourself to focus on the conversation. Let human touch take priority over screen touch.
- Quality of sleep is required for mental health. Looking at TV, the internet, social media, and WhatsApp chats before sleep will affect the quality of sleep. Keep yourself away from all the gadgets for at least 30 minutes before you sleep.
- Identify time wasters and decide on the extent in terms of duration of usage of the internet social media per day.
- Like regular fasting, start practicing a digital detox schedule. Say no to the usage of social media and internet for 8 hours on Sunday or after 8 pm on daily basis. Overindulgence in mobile and social media has been reported to cause physical inactivity, obesity, decreased quality of sleep, social incompatibility, anxiety, and aggressive behaviour.
- Delete all the Apps on the mobile that will not support your productivity.
- Identify zones in the house like bedroom and kitchen where mobiles or any digital gadgets do not find an entry.
- A ship in the sea is fully surrounded by salty water. This water is of no use for the people inside the ship unless it is processed to get drinking water. Likewise, we are flooded today with lots of information. Learn to process it properly to get what you want for your growth.
- Keep a watch on children's usage of mobile and control their usage. They will get addicted faster.

How you use technology is a choice. Using it wisely as an enabler will make you more productive. Anything in excess is poison.

My top three improvement action points

1.

2.

3.

46

KNOW THE PATH AND WALK THE PATH

> *If you are walking down the right path and you're willing to keep walking eventually you'll progress*
> — **Barack Obama**

So much has been talked about enlightenment in Hinduism, in which it is said that there are four paths for the aspirants to enlightenment. They are Karma Yoga (the path of action), Bhakti Yoga (the path of devotion), Raja Yoga (the path of meditation) and Jnana Yoga (the path of knowledge). Aspirants can select any of these paths, based on their liking, to reach the destination.

Likewise, each person has his own path in life, and no two paths are exactly alike. To be successful, whatever you have defined as success, following these aspects will support you:

A. Knowing the path
B. Preparing for the path
C. Walking the path

Knowing the path

Which path do you want to take? Why do you want to take that path? What is your goal in life? Where do you want to reach and by when? What is your plan to get there? What actions are required to be taken?

Before deciding to climb Mount Everest, first, ask yourself why you want to climb the mountain and from where you will start, which route you will take for climbing, what your endpoint is, in which season you want to climb.

In the context of an organization, what is your vision? What is the purpose or mission of the organization? What values are to be carried along the path? Who should come along with you on your journey? What strategy will you have to reach your vision?

Preparing for the path

Having decided to climb Mount Everest, would you simply go near the base and start climbing? It will be a disaster. What preparations are required for the journey? What physical fitness is required and how do you build that? What types of foods are required and how much to carry? What would be the weather conditions and what type of clothes are required and how many? What types of medicines and supplements are required? How many oxygen cans are required to manage in high altitudes? What guidelines are to be followed should there be an emergency on the way? Which of the locals help you in case of emergency? Which type of shoes are required? What could the terrain be like? What practices do you need like climbing small mountains?

In the context of an organization, what structure do you need to develop to reach the vision? Which skills and competencies are required to be developed in the organization? What should be your next milestone? What type of measurements would you choose to know the extent of your walk on the path? What obstacles and risks may come up in the path? What preparations are required to mitigate those risks? What resources are required? Whom can you consult for any inputs?

Walking the path

Real success is walking the path, and it is about acting. Knowing and preparing have no meaning unless you start walking. You may not see the top of Mount Everest, though you have an idea of the path. Your visibility will be only one hundred meters. Cover that with care and focus, and you will see the path of the next stretch. Mentally, be ready for sudden changes of weather and tough terrain. Go further without giving up.

Swami Vivekananda rightly said, "If there are no obstacles on your path, check whether you are on the right path."

Terry Fox of Canada, a cancer research activist who had lost one leg for osteosarcoma and fitted with an artificial leg, decided to walk across Canada, collecting one dollar per person on the way of his marathon walk all over the country to raise funds for cancer research. When he was interviewed and asked how he could do that, he said his focus on the walk was only till the next lamp post. Once he reached there, he would focus on the next post.

In the context of an organization, break the goal into small bits and take one step at a time to complete. Have a review to see where you have reached and where you should have been. Work on this gap so that you keep up with the final timeline. Do not give up due to challenges and obstacles on the way which are bound to come up.

I met an MD of a family-owned business. He had built the company from scratch, dedicating almost his whole life. He had only one son. As the son was not brought into business thinking early in childhood, he was more inclined to be an employee of a multinational company and joined there. He chose a different path. The father wanted his son to come and walk on the well-laid path he built over decades. Finally, with reluctance, the son came when the father became old. The father would have done better by convincing his son early to take the path he built for decades and teaching him how to walk the path. With the help of mentors, the son got to know the path, prepared for the walk and started moving in the path. The journey was not smooth for him in the initial few years.

Following these **6Ps** will help you walk better in the path you have decided.

Priority – Be clear on the selection of the path among many other options you might have.

Purpose – Have clarity on why you chose this specific path and the meaning that it brings to you. The choice should be yours.

Plan – Plan well for short-term, medium-term, and long-term walks on the path. Define clear milestones along the path.

Prepare – Spend time on this including mental preparation to face the challenges on the way.

Practice – Start at a slow pace and with small steps initially. With practice, you can leap later.

Perform – With the completion of the above steps, it should be easy to move further in your path. Be consistent in your efforts. Enjoy the journey in your path.

Have you decided on your path?

My top three improvement action points

1.

2.

3.

47

INCREASE ROTI OF THE MEETINGS

People who enjoy meetings should not be in charge of anything

– Thomas Sowell

All of us who are in offices and companies are very familiar with meetings and their objectives. Let us be honest. Are we really getting the desired outcomes from the meetings? What should be the core purpose of the meetings? Are our meetings productive? How to make them more effective?

Some people who are not really connected with the agenda of the meeting still participate in the meeting as it is a wonderful place for relaxation. They have the chance to enjoy some snacks or drinks and watch the drama going on. Many times, the outcome of the meeting will be coming out of the meeting. Hours will be lost to make the minutes of the meeting. Some people being in the meeting itself is an obstruction. They tend to harp on the problems rather than trying to find ways for the solution.

I saw a wonderful board outside of a meeting room in a company in bold letters that read, "Before entering the meeting room, be clear whether you are part of the problem or of the solution."

The core purpose of the meeting is not to share the status of various issues with the participants but to brainstorm, discuss critical issues, resolve conflicts, share vital information or arrive at decisions to take up the next actions. Time must be used to reflect on the gap between where we are and where we should have been. Instead of this, if we focus on whether someone has done the task agreed upon or not, the effectiveness of the meeting will come down. The meeting is not a replacement for those things that can be solved by email, telephone or other means. The focus should be on the return for the investments (ROI) done in terms of time. We may call this ROTI—**R**eturn **O**n **T**ime **I**nvested. What could be the ways to make meetings more meaningful and productive to increase ROTI:

If you are the host of the meeting,
- Ensure that there is a clear agenda and objective.
- Inform participants well in time.
- Invite only those who are really needed.
- Define start and end time.
- Stick to the agenda and be focused.
- Do not allow diversions.
- See if a standing meeting is possible to cut short the time.
- Involve all participants in discussions to speak their mind
- Do not fix a meeting that lasts hours. Participants will lose focus. Recommend a maximum of 1 hour.
- Use the 'parking lot' concept to note down points that are not relevant to this meeting but are to be dealt with separately.
- Summarise the points at the end of the meeting with action points, including who will carry out, the due date for completion and when the review will happen. Participants should leave with full clarity on what each will do next. ROTI of a meeting is low if participants say at the end, "I will look into it," "I will try," or "I will discuss next time." Such vague expressions will not lead to any progress.

- In review meetings, let focus be on facts rather than opinions, stories and assumptions
- Do not dwell too much on the past. Take lessons and focus on what is to be done next.
- Once in a way, evaluate the quality of the meeting with inputs from participants to make it better next time.
- In a project review, the focus should be on actions that will lead to progress instead of a dry discussion on status and numbers. Harping too much on the past is not productive.

Take care of these points as a participant--
- Go with the preparations for the meeting, including the points you would like to contribute, points to get clarified and actions taken by you from the previous meeting minutes, if any. It is an opportunity to practice your expression.
- Be open-minded to absorb the views of other participants. Listen attentively when others speak without interrupting.
- Challenge the ideas or points of others without attacking the person.
- Respect timings and be punctual. Be there 5 minutes early. If you go late, it is disrespectful to others. If delayed for a specific reason, inform the organizer in advance.
- If the topic is not relevant to you and if you are not contributing, politely refuse to attend, giving the reason to the organizer.
- Avoid dominating in the meeting. With this, others will not put forth their views properly.
- When you are attending a meeting with a specific problem of yours, go with a proposal of solutions instead of a problem. Be concise, clear, and complete with data.
- Be attentive fully in the meeting and avoid distractions from mobile or laptop.
- Do not indulge in cross-discussions which will distract others.

- If a point is not clear, do not hesitate to ask questions to get clarified.
- Note down the actions you agreed to do.
- After the meeting, ensure that the actions agreed by you are completed within the time frame. Do not necessitate someone to follow up with you on this.
- If your topic is very small in a lengthy meeting, seek the permission of the chairperson to take up your point first so that you can leave the meeting early.
- Follow other etiquette of meetings such as dressing style, greetings and so on.

In a company, I saw that there was a daily review meeting of one hour daily. This was meant to review the previous day's work in terms of whether targets were met and, if not, what is the reason. I observed that the focus was on blaming who was responsible for the shortfall rather than on core issues of root causes and prevention steps to avoid reoccurrence. With this, the meeting was not effective and was done mechanically. When I attended this meeting once, I suggested that they have a goal to reduce the duration of the meeting or eliminate the meetings completely. When there were curious looks at my suggestion, I said if everybody plays their role well daily, there is no need for a review meeting. Instead of this, the goal was to have a meeting daily. The meeting is a means to the end and not the end itself.

It may be a good idea to calculate the cost of each meeting considering the duration of the meeting, how many attended and their hourly rate. By recording and monitoring this monthly, people will be more conscious of the cost of meeting and the corresponding value that came out.

By following the above disciplines, the productivity of meetings can be enhanced. You can make untrue a typical saying on meeting as a place where productivity goes to die. If not managed, the meeting will end up with a lot of wasted time. Work on increasing the ROTI of meetings to be more productive.

My top three improvement action points

1.

2.

3.

48

WAYS TO OVERCOME NEGATIVITY

Negativity is the enemy of creativity
                                         – **David Lynch**

Everything happens twice. First in our mind and later physically. Negative thoughts towards the actions and results can have an impact on actual results.

"Having a positive mental attitude is asking how something can be done rather than saying it can't be done," says Bo Bennett, a social psychologist. Negativity has a serious impact on productivity. It may be a thought, feeling or expression of words. When we have negativity in our minds, the world also looks like that. After all, we see the world and surroundings as per our mental framework and not as they are. When we fail in a task, we tend to think of some failure in our next task as well.

One person was going to heaven. On the way, he comes across a wonderful tree that could give him everything he thinks in his mind. Having tired from the journey, he thinks of good food. All sorts of wonderful and fresh foods appear instantaneously. After eating, he wishes for a comfortable place to rest. That was fulfilled. While he was busy asking for more things, suddenly he doubted whether this could be an act of a ghost. Soon, many ghosts appeared dancing. Now, this person starts fearing what to do if the ghosts eat him, which was granted. That was the end of him.

Please do an exercise. Open today's newspaper and highlight all positive news items with green colour and all negative news items with red colour. Which colour would you see predominantly? Obviously, it's a more of red colour. Why? Negativity spreads faster, and the media uses this effectively. Negativity can be compared to an ocean. The ship needs an ocean to sail through. But the ship will sink if it allows the surrounding water to get in. Similarly, we may be surrounded by negativity, but if we care not to allow this to enter our minds, we can sail well in life.

At the end of each day, as a part of reflection, write down all the good things that happened and all the negative things that happened. Most days, more positive things only happen, but unfortunately, our mind is conditioned to look at only the negative aspects of the day. As you observe this, learn to focus only on the positive aspects of the day. I came across an exercise in training. The trainer wrote a few black dots on the whiteboard and asked the participants to share what they saw on the board. The majority said that they saw a number of black spots and spoke about their size, how they spoiled the beauty of the board and so on. Later, the trainer asked them to reflect on why they did not appreciate the white portion of the board which was 99%+. Mind conditioning had made participants to focus on things which are not nice. Change the perspective.

Face the negative situations with a positive mindset. Thinking positively without taking action will not give results. A positive mindset gives the energy to face challenges and negative situations as well. Positive thinking and actions will not guarantee success but will increase the probability of success. On the other hand, negative thinking will lead to failure for sure. With negative thinking, others may not appreciate your work, and results may not come. You may not focus hundred percent on the job you are engaged with hampering the result. To overcome negativity, you need to practice a few things. Some of these could be:

- Identify the source of negativity. It could be social media, TV, newspaper, or some of your contacts. Think about the reduction of these external sources of negativity.
- Identify positive things in a situation. When you fail, instead of being negative, ask yourself what you can learn from the situation and what actions can be taken in the future.
- Use the support of friends, parents, and mentors to overcome negativity with their feedback.
- Too much idle time is not good. The devil called negativity will enter your mind easily when you are lazy and idle. Stop thinking of things that do not exist.
- You may have a feeling that people may be thinking negatively about your work. Remember that everyone is busy with their own job and will not have time to think about yours.
- Do not brood too much about your mistakes. Be compassionate to yourself. Look at the positive side and keep moving.
- Do not try to be a perfectionist, and do not expect that everything you do should yield positive results.
- Do not get into paralysis of analysis. Too much thinking typically leads to seeing the negative side.
- Develop the mindset to be present in this current moment, delinking the past and future.
- Things like yoga, breathing exercises, workouts, affirmations, visualisation, and relaxation techniques will help a lot in overcoming negativity.
- Believe in your strengths instead of grumbling over weaknesses.
- To overcome fear, think of the worst that can happen to you and be ready for that.

- Think of positive things that happened in your life. Be grateful for these.
- Spend more time with people who are optimistic about life.
- Read motivational books to get inspired to reduce negative thoughts.
- Regrets and worries make you think negatively. Try fixing expiry dates for those and move on.
- Write down the negative thoughts that come up frequently and review them by yourself. Allocate a time daily for this. You will gain control over them slowly. It is a very powerful technique.

Your productivity will be hampered by negative thinking. You are the first victim of your negativity. The mind cannot remain a vacuum. It can hold on to only one thing at a time. Push with positive thoughts consistently to drive out negativity. Mind is like a field. If you don't take care to cultivate the plants you want, you will end up with weeds of negativity, which will grow by themselves with minimum or no nourishment. Negative thoughts are like junk foods, which are not good for the health. Work on this to minimise or avoid.

My top three improvement action points

1.

2.

3.

49

CLING TO ROUTINES

> *You will never change your life until you change something you do daily. The secret to your success is found in your daily routine*
> — **John C. Maxwell**

All of you are aware that for success, along with talent, hard work is required. No great thing is ever achieved by anyone without putting in sufficient hours of effort. A scientific study done in Germany among violists proved that the best among them was the one who had practised more than the others in terms of the number of years and that too consistently. The power of routine is the secret of success, which will not be visible to others. To be a good musician, you need to practice daily, even if you think that you have achieved excellence in the domain. It is not enough to play musical instruments mechanically for hours daily. You need to push yourself to learn new, difficult things, get feedback by playing before others, learn from previous mistakes and think of ways to improve. This deliberate practice helps you to develop competency. If you do it the same way as you have been doing routinely, it will not give great results.

During Corona pandemic, I was attending online yoga sessions. The teacher started with only one thing first. To make yoga a routine by showing up everyday morning at 6:30 am and involve in some body movements for 45 minutes. Initially, he did not insist on discipline, ways to breathe during exercises, usage of the mat, food discipline, etc. He knew that the biggest challenge to continuing the practice of yoga was the inability to cling to daily routines. Over the period, as participants saw the benefit of routine, he slowly started improving postures, breathing and so on.

In my earlier experience of yoga with another, the teacher was too strict, imposing so many disciplines before coming for the session. This made me difficult to comply with, and slowly, I started skipping the routines and ultimately, I stopped going to the session. Start with routine first without bothering about the quality and other things. The latter will come gradually. Regular practice through routines leads to the development of skills and not the other way around. Start small, even imperfectly.

In one mentoring session with a manager of a company, I observed that he had challenges connecting with his team members and peers. He also realised this, which was hampering the results. I suggested he start spending 15 minutes at least with one of his team members talking about the difficulties of the person, his or her aspirations, family situations, any support needed and ways to collaborate. I also cautioned not to expect any results and not to bother too much with the quality of discussions. In a few months, he started realising the power of the routine started. If you want to develop competency, reflect on what daily routines and practices are needed to achieve the level of competence you need.

The advantage of clinging to a routine is that your mind will be ready at that time to absorb it. We are often engaged in a task, not taking the mind along. By sticking to a routine over a period, you would be better than a person with more abilities and experience. You are what you repeatedly do, and success is the sum of all small efforts put in daily.

Cling to Routines

When Bruce Lee, the king of Kung-Fu, was asked in an interview as to who he is afraid of as an opponent, he said, "I am not worried about a person who knows thousands of tricks, but I am worried about a person who has practiced one trick thousand times."

Many religions prescribe routine. In Sanskrit, it is called *Dinacharya*. Routines set a direction. Some people will find it difficult to stick to routines as growth is not visible on a daily basis. A stone is broken by the last stroke of a hammer. This doesn't mean that the initial strokes were useless. Start planting seeds daily without thinking about harvest. Some points to reflect on and follow routines to gain benefits are:

- Be clear about what routines are suited for you to reach the destination or goal you have decided. Do not follow just because someone else is doing it. It should fit into your schedule and be important for you. For example, if you want to be successful in marketing, call or interact with new potential customers daily.
- Do not be in routine mechanically but push yourself to improve each day through deliberate practice.
- Budget a time for practicing routine.
- What is done consistently on a daily basis, even imperfectly, yields better results than the one done perfectly once in a way.
- What question are you posing to yourself daily to push yourself? Do you have the habit of introspecting often? If not, you should develop a routine for reflection.
- Winston Churchill used to spend morning hours daily thinking and decision-making to set a tone for a productive day. Gandhiji had a routine of early morning prayer, writing and walking.
- Routines need not have to be daily but can be weekly or monthly. It is about the rhythm.

- Routines could be related to knowledge & skill development, career progress, physical fitness, eating and drinking, relaxation, entertainment, hobbies, building relationships, prayer, dairy or journal writing and so on.
- Identify and nurture your NMWs, i.e., No Matter What. Daily NMW routines are like meditation, exercise, walking, being with nature, reading, reflection and so on. You are what you practice.

Practicing a routine is powerful in boosting productivity.

Good to reflect daily on the words of Joe Louis, a professional American boxer, "A champion doesn't become a champion in the ring. He is merely recognized in the ring. His becoming happens during his daily routine." Routines lead to habits. Go ahead and identify a few routines consciously that fit you to develop positive habits and start practicing them.

My top three improvement action points

1.

2.

3.

50
OVERCOMING LAZINESS

Laziness is nothing more than the habit of resting before you get tired
— **Jules Renard**

In my training sessions, participants invariably list laziness as one of the root causes for postponing their actions and not being able to be productive. The alternate word used for laziness is sloth, meaning reluctance to work or to make an effort. When we discuss further, many start justifying laziness as a part of their personality and something not possible to overcome. Their mind is conditioned to think that laziness is something they must live with forever. Have you come across persons who set up alarm clocks to get up early in the morning but end up hitting the snooze button of the alarm a few times before getting up much later? Their day starts with the breaking of their own promise because of laziness. This habit, if it goes on for a longer period, gives an identity that they are lazy, and the same aspects get reflected in their other activities.

Laziness may develop because of hindrances to change. Other typical reasons are fear, the force of old habits and negative beliefs. Lazy persons find immediate gratification by escaping to do something without realising that they will pay for it later. One such payment is regret. In my student days, I was lazy to learn to swim, though I had many opportunities. I felt happy escaping classes. I was looking for days when there were no swimming classes. I realised my mistake much later in life.

Everyone is lazy at some time or the other. That is not an issue. But being lazy most of the time or being lazy when real actions are required comes in the way of your success or achievement.

What could be the real reason for being lazy? Mostly, it is related to the type of action to be taken next. If the action is boring, you do not like it, or it is something thrust on you heavily, you tend to demonstrate laziness to escape at least temporarily from those actions. My wife believed that learning some musical instruments is good for children as she herself had learnt music. She forced my son to learn to play the keyboard. Out of pressure from the teacher and us, he started going to classes. He did well initially and must have realised that it was not his cup of tea. Slowly, he started finding excuses to skip classes and miss practices. He would be very happy when the teacher was out of the station. We started thinking that he may be lazy because he didn't learn music. But we found out in later days that the same boy would spend time beyond midnight studying his favourite subject, Physics. Now, can we call him a lazy person?

Would you be too lazy to get up if you must catch up on an early morning flight? The answer is a definitive no. This is because if you miss the flight, being lazy, you will lose big money. In this case, you tend to get up much early, keeping a buffer time to make sure you do not miss the flight. What drove you here not to be lazy is the importance of the task.

You can overcome laziness if you identify the importance or the criticality of the task you need to take. Or make the task so interesting for you, in which case, you don't want to miss acting. For example, if you are too lazy to take a morning walk, make your walking interesting by finding a walking partner to chat with or having a nice coffee in a nearby restaurant after the walk. I have overcome the laziness of getting up at 5 am every day by desiring to drink my beloved black coffee as the first thing early in the morning.

You tend to be lazy and get bored when you do not have a purpose or goal. Before going to bed, write down all the key tasks and goals you want to achieve the next day. You will have reason to get up in time and to engage in those tasks you planned. When you complete those tasks, give a pat to yourself and that will be a motivation for you to take up the next task without being lazy. Start with small tasks to take action and complete. Motivation will pave the way to go further. The domino effect will work to take up bigger tasks without being lazy.

Another way to overcome laziness is to think of the implications of being lazy. This reflection on your choice and the consequences will support you in shedding off layers of laziness.

Find an accountability partner who can hold you accountable. He or she can be a colleague, friend or family member. With this, you will be more conscious of not being lazy.

Laziness is likely to occur when you are not clear about what to do. Goal setting helps. Goals will enable you to set a plan of action, and you are less likely to be lazy.

Strong routines developed as habits will reduce your laziness. Habits will become part and parcel of you, and you need not have to spend much energy to motivate yourself daily. But be ready to be uncomfortable while forming habits.

The Holy Bible says that a lazy man's desire remains unsatisfied while diligent people gain wealth and prosperity. In Buddhism, laziness is defined as clinging to unwholesome activities such as lying down and procrastinating and not being enthusiastic about or engaging in virtuous activities.

If there were a tablet to overcome laziness, there would have been a huge business for this product. Unfortunately, there is no such ready medicine. The current remedy is identifying the importance of the task, making the task interesting and finding a goal or purpose for the task. Identify first which actions and situations make you lazy to address.

As rightly said by someone, "Success is not easy, and it is certainly not for the lazy." Start working on your identity by taking up a small action which you postponed for the reason of laziness. Start following the tagline of Nike Shoes, 'Just do it', whenever you feel lazy to start. Wish you a successful day without laziness.

My top three improvement action points

1.

2.

3.

51

DO NOT LOSE THE PERSON

You don't know who is important to you until you actually lose them

– Mahatma Gandhi

Sudeep (name changed) is a well-qualified and experienced person. As a freelancer, he was good at technical training. I really liked his approach and conduct of some of the training sessions on my behalf. He used to interact with me on various subjects and meet me once in a way. On one occasion, I fixed his training for another customer, where his expertise was higher than mine. Being a front end to customers, I coordinated the outline of the program, duration, date, commercials and so on. In every interaction, he was in the loop, as I believed in transparency. Everything went well initially. The customer suddenly started asking about changes in dates on short notice and the outline. Sudeep got irritated with the behaviour of the customer. I tried to convince him, saying that we have no control over what the customer does as I knew that the HR person of the customer was also under various compulsions.

In earlier programs, where everything sailed well, there were no issues with Sudeep. I failed to understand what made him behave differently in this case. He started writing to customers unprofessionally, blaming them for attaching no value to the knowledge. The customer also got irritated, and the program was cancelled. I tried my best to pacify Sudeep from my long experience in dealing with customers, but it was of no use. He stopped responding to my messages and calls. I left him to fend for himself at that stage and moved further with the customer by doing that training myself. Sudeep took extreme steps to lose the relationship and the person. He could have told me politely if he was not happy with the customer's behaviour, and we could have jointly resolved. This did not happen. He reacted quickly without understanding the realities. He lost many other opportunities which I and the customer were planning for him.

This incident made me reflect on whether I did anything wrong in dealing with him. I did not find any. I personally believe that a person is more important than transactions. I tried all means to bring him back, but that did not happen. Everyone has a choice to do what he or she thinks is right or wrong. As a professional, he could have handled the situation well. Anyway, it was his choice. He was not willing to listen to me. I would have been happy if he had given feedback on my approach to correct the relationship. That did not happen. I had to leave him in further interactions. I had to lose him as the customer also was not willing to work with him. Such situations happen. Looking at further opportunities that came up later for him, for which he was not considered, I realised that he lost me more than I lost him. Do not be like Sudeep, and don't lose people easily. Building a relationship takes years, but breaking takes minutes.

I went with my daughter to buy a mobile phone in a well-known shop. They had many varieties, and the price also was reasonable compared to their competitors. My daughter could not decide to buy one at that time as she wanted to explore a little more about the features of the gadget. Sensing that we would not buy at our visit, the salesperson who was attending to us started behaving a little differently. We could see that in his body language. Next time, my daughter did not allow me to go to this shop. The shop lost a customer forever. Every interaction or dealing with the customer may not go in your favour but you have to make sure that customer experience in each touch point is positive. If the relationship is good, the customer comes back when the need arises.

Benjamin Franklin, who was a strong believer in the importance of customer service, gave key words of advice to sellers, "If customers see your goods and undervalue them, endeavour to convince them of their mistake, but do not affront them; do not be rude in your answers, but with patience hear, and with meekness give an answer, for if you affront in a small matter, it may hinder you from a future good customer. They may think you are expensive in the articles they want, but going to another may find it not so, and probably may return. However, if you behave rude and affronting, there is no hope either of returning or their future custom." Do not be an opportunist with a thinking that you want to gain in every interaction with others.

When the nail grows, we cut them and not our fingers. Ego and enmity are like nails. Keep trimming them instead of cutting relationships and people. Ending a relationship is a last resort when all other means to bring it back do not work.

What Franklin said in short was, "Be ready to lose the business or transaction but not the person and relationship." If you have to break with a person, do it gracefully so that you can go back to him or her if needed. Never burn the bridge. For the people leaving an organization for various reasons, tell them to exit the organization and people gracefully without hurting anyone or spoiling the relationship. The world is round, and you will never know whom you will meet again in a different context. Leave the business but not the people.

My top three improvement action points

1.

2.

3.

52

TAKE RESPONSIBILITY

When you react, you are giving away your power. When you respond, you are staying in control of yourself
— **Bob Proctor**

It was a Sunday evening. While watching TV, Lokesh was thinking about why weekends are so short and why Monday comes so quickly. He was one among many who was looking for next weekend and especially Fridays to say, "Thank God, it is Friday." Two hours later, Lokesh got a call from his boss saying that the next day, on Monday, an important potential customer was coming to the office by 9 am, and he should put up the best presentation to them. Lokesh quickly but reluctantly pulls out his laptop to prepare a presentation with a feeling that Monday has already started. This work goes on for a few hours till midnight, and he went to sleep after setting an alarm for 7 am. He missed dinner that evening.

The alarm rang at 7.30 am, and Lokesh realised that the alarm clock was half an hour slower than the actual time. He rushed to the bathroom only to find it was occupied by his daughter. He started shouting at his daughter for taking a long time. To present himself well before the potential customer, he looked for a nice shirt and observed that it was not ironed. He ironed it, gulped breakfast, and rushed to see that his car was parked in front of another car by his son the previous day. He cursed his son for parking wrongly. It took another 30 minutes to pull out his car, and he started rushing to the office. His drive was reckless to save the lost time, and he was totally tense. Typical of Monday morning, there was unusual traffic, and by the time he reached the office, it was 10 am.

As he entered the office, Lokesh could see the frustration of the boss in his body language. Boss scolded Lokesh for being so irresponsible and shouted about how it had affected the company's image before the prospective customer. The day started for Lokesh, and he was grumbling the whole day, blaming many people and situations, including his bad time. No explanation is needed to narrate how his day was and what his achievements were on that day.

Who is responsible for this?

- Was it because it was a Monday?
- His son parked wrongly.
- His daughter occupied the bathroom.
- The shirts were not ironed.
- The alarm that woke him up half an hour later.
- The customer who gave short notice to visit.
- The boss agreed to a meeting on short notice.
- Traffic condition
- It was a bad time for Lokesh

Or was it Lokesh himself?

Situations and circumstances keep coming. Many times, you may not have control over them. You have a choice whether to react or respond to those. The reaction is instantaneous, with no thoughts involved and emotion based. The response is logical, thought over and with a pause. In the pause, take a deep breath, resist the urge to act impulsively, observe your feelings quickly, put your ego aside and think through the consequences. With reaction, the outcome may not be wanted, but with the response, the outcome can be favourable. The outcome is dependent on responding or reacting to the event.

Once, my boss scolded me badly for an issue for which I was not responsible. He did so because of a communication gap. I also shouted at him in a reactive mode, and the consequence was a dent in our relationship later. I realised my mistake after weeks. I could have listened to him holding back my emotions and could have gone back to him on the next day when his negative emotion was low to find out what made him scold me, and I could have given a proper explanation. But the damage was done already. Scars of outcomes of reaction will stay for too long.

Wayne Dyer, an American self-help author, said, "How people treat you is their Karma. How you react is yours". Pause before judging, assuming, accusing, complaining, blaming, pinpointing, and reacting. You will avoid lots of regrets later.

If you must work with a highly reactive person, watch and be careful about your words and actions. If you also react instead of responding, it will be like pouring ghee into the fire to flare up. You have control to change yourself rather than expecting others to change.

In between a lady's party in a restaurant, a cockroach came from nowhere and landed on a lady. She screamed and created a scene there, making everybody else panic and spoil the spirit of the party. In the process, the cockroach flew and landed on the shirt of a waiter. He picked it up, went outside, threw it, and he continued his job. The lady reacted, and the waiter responded.

In the above situation, what could Lokesh have done differently to achieve the outcome of making a good presentation to the prospective customer at 9 am on Monday? He could have used the technique of **PEACE**. This may not give a guaranteed outcome, but it surely increases the probability of a positive outcome, and you get the satisfaction that you did your best in the given circumstances.

- **P**ause – Before jumping to preparing the presentation the previous night, he could have paused a few minutes to see what all is required to be at 9 am tomorrow, work backwards and seek support from others.
- **E**valuating - the situation and seeing how best he could respond.
- **A**wareness – of feelings and agitation going on at that moment within himself and to address them with empowering thoughts.
- **C**alming down by taking deep breaths, having dinner and preparing the mind
- **E**mpathizing by putting himself in his boss's shoes and trying to understand the compulsions he may have to disturb on Sunday night.

Responsibility is a combination of RESPONSE and ABILITY. Increase your ability to respond to the situation in a better way. Take responsibility to bring those in control which can be controlled. Then, you will see things falling into place the way you want.

My top three improvement action points

1.

2.

3.

EPILOGUE

Soft factors drive hard results. Repeated practices are required to master soft aspects and anything related to the mind. A renowned executive coach, Marshall Gold Smith, talks about expensive watches that don't show the right time without the right battery. Facilities and resources can be exploited fully in the best way with the right human element and the personal productivity of those involved. Focusing on personal productivity, one can exploit, to a great extent, inner potential.

Many blocks are needed to be fully productive. You can start preparing your own castle of personal productivity by correctly using the fifty-two blocks explained in the book. You also would have noticed the linkage of one block to another. For example, effective time utilization is linked to procrastination, excuses, and laziness.

Take one block at a time and understand the theoretical framework, stimulating you to draw your own action plan. Note down other insights you get by reading each chapter. Meticulously execute through consistent practices until they become second nature. You can start immediately, even in a small way, without further delay.

Do not underestimate the power of reflection. Daily practice helps you understand where you are, what is going on in your mind, how your practices are giving results, and what you should do next.

Reading and understanding without corresponding actions of principles will not help you. Medicines will work only if taken.

Things will work only if you work on it. No thoughtful efforts will go awaste.

Thank you for picking up the book and reading it completely. I appreciate your commitment to improving your productivity, which will lead to your personal growth. I wish you all the best for your efforts, and I hope you will emerge as a fulfilled person. Good luck.

PROFILE OF THE AUTHOR, P. S. SATISH

An MTech in engineering from the Indian Institute of Technology (IIT), Chennai, P. S. Satish is a corporate trainer, mentor, and management consultant for manufacturing industries and engineering institutions. He has been associated with manufacturing industries for more than three decades and close to a decade with educational institutes.

For five years, as a professor of practice at Ramaiah University of Applied Sciences, Bengaluru, he guided many students during their master's degree in engineering.

He has headed the global sourcing division of the company Robert Bosch for close to 10 years, visited over 25+ countries and had the opportunity to interact with hundreds of companies globally and in India. He worked in various functions in the company before deciding to leave the corporate world more than a decade ago to pursue his passion for training, mentoring, and writing.

Currently, he enjoys running a service company under the name of **S**araswati **I**ndustrial **S**ervices (SIS) in Bengaluru. He believes strongly from his observations that companies suffer more from human challenges than the challenges posed by the market dynamics, and all challenges, whether at the professional or personal level, can be addressed by self-development. He enjoys developing people and industries, and with this, he has expanded the acronym of his company, SIS, to **S**haring and **S**haping of **I**ndividuals, **I**ndustries, and **I**nstitutions.

He is on the editorial advisory board of an industrial magazine, *Machine Maker*, and has published more than 75 articles related to the improvement of thinking, management, business processes, and people in manufacturing industries.

With a deep passion for training, speaking, and writing, he regularly visits colleges and industries to guide students, employees, entrepreneurs, and businessmen to help them realize their full potential. He enthusiastically mentors budding entrepreneurs & people aspiring to grow and loves to see them grow. As a corporate trainer, he has developed and delivered 50+ training modules covering various aspects of manufacturing industries.

He has other published books: *Knowing Is Not Same as Doing, The Great Entrepreneur Blueprint – 52 Dimensions* and *Sanjeevana* (in Kannada Language). His hobbies include reading, speaking, and writing in English and Kannada. He can be reached through WhatsApp at +91-9845043202.

OTHER BOOKS BY P.S.SATISH

www.ingramcontent.com/pod-product-compliance
Lightning Source LLC
LaVergne TN
LVHW041700070526
838199LV00045B/1138